*Jews and the American Revolution*

# Jews and the American Revolution: Haym Salomon and Others

*by*
## Laurens R. Schwartz

WITH A FOREWORD
BY ARNO PENZIAS

McFarland & Company, Inc., Publishers
*Jefferson, North Carolina, and London*

Illustrations (pages 30, 38, two on 49, 62, 80, 88, two on 96, 100) courtesy of the New York Public Library, Rare Books Division.

**Library of Congress Cataloguing-in-Publication Data**

Schwartz, Laurens R.
  *Jews and the American Revolution.*

  Bibliography: p. 159
  Includes index.
  1. Salomon, Haym, 1740–1785.  2. United States—
History—Revolution, 1775–1783—Biography.  3. United
States—History—Revolution, 1775–1783—Participation,
Jewish.  4. Jews—United States—Biography.  I. Title.
E302.6.S17S39  1987      973.3'092'4 [B]      85-43590

ISBN  0-89950-220-2 (acid-free natural paper) ∞

Printed in the United States of America.

McFarland   Box 611   Jefferson NC 28640

For Dahlia, and my predecessors

# Table of Contents

# Acknowledgments

I wish to thank Maxwell Whiteman, a fine historian specializing in the history of Jews in Philadelphia, for his advice, suggestions, leads and overall kindness. The New York Public Library, Rare Books and Manuscript Divisions, for opening their dusty metal gratings so I could gain access to original materials. The Yivo Institute of New York, The Historical Society of Pennsylvania, a certain Masonic repository, the Surrogate's Court of New York City, and a number of synagogues for permitting me to poke around in nooks and crannies. The American Jewish Historical Society, and its librarian, Dr. Nathan M. Kaganoff, with whom I exchanged documents and debated the era. And Rabbis interested in helping a Jew who had forgotten his Hebrew.

I also wish to thank Dr. Arno Penzias, a laureate of the most humane order, for his suggestions and prefatory comments; and Robert Foah of Atlanta Audio-Visuals for taking time out to photograph the documents included in this book, often under dire circumstances. Additional gratitude is due to

Belle Shuller, for her support and broad knowledge of Jewish lore and history; my parents, in-laws and wife, for their love; all the dogs I have had who have devoted themselves to lowering my blood pressure; and, most particularly, to my daughter, Dahlia, who represents a new generation combining heritage and hope.

Laurens R. Schwartz
New York City

# Foreword

I confess to having something of a blind spot when it comes to the American Revolution. Like most of us, I first learned about it in elementary school — it came just a little after the story of the Pilgrims. It was filled with two-dimensional characters who walked around in powdered wigs and never told a lie. Finally, in adulthood, I came to appreciate the people that founded this country, the genius of Jefferson, the earthy humanity and ingenuity of Benjamin Franklin, and, with this volume, the spirit of Haym Salomon and his Jewish contemporaries.

Still, attitudes formed in childhood are hard to expunge. My perception of Haym Salomon has given me the most trouble. As a kid who grew up in the 1940s — a young refugee desperately wanted to be an American — I looked for heroes to identify with wherever I could find them. Next to the romantic popular figures of Washington, Lafayette, Pulaski, and von Steuben, the name Haym Salomon seemed to be a kind of consolation prize for the Jewish children. Those were the days, before the State of Israel was created, when it was taken for granted by everybody (including us, I'm afraid), that Jews just didn't make good soldiers and stood in the background of armed conflicts. There were the generals, presumably fighting bravely in battle, and then there were Haym Salomon and other Jews, staying at home or in a comfortable bank somewhere, making sure that the money in the till matched the money in the ledgers. The ubiquitous, stereotyped money lenders.

Until the day I picked up this book, my picture of Haym Salomon remained with me as a residue of my refugee status in America. Now, having read of the dangers he faced and the risks he took, I see him in a new light. We learn in the opening chapter that Salomon had been imprisoned as a rebel sympathizer early in the British occupation of New York, confined to a notorious prison in which torture was the rule of the day and death often welcomed. He gained a parole of sorts because of his facility for foreign languages. Despite the risk of discovery, reimprisonment and all its consequences, he worked frantically to advance the rebel cause, in a myriad of ways — persuading others, helping prisoners to escape, serving as agent provocateur, saboteur, and anything else he could do.

Finally forced to flee New York, he established himself in Philadelphia,where he struggled to keep the Continental Congress, and himself, just this side of bankruptcy. The struggle was exacerbated by petty quarrels, personal vanity and simple greed, enough to discourage all but the most deeply committed. Throughout it all, Salomon remained faithful to the idea of the nation he was helping to build.

Somehow, this passionate idealism must have had its origins in an early life marked by the painful experiences which were the common lot of European Jews in that age. Here, in the new world, a new set of ideas would replace what he had left behind in the old world. As the author puts it, "a social compact

... between man and government drawn from certain rights which could not be taken away." Perhaps we can see something of his readiness to accept such a compact by examining the other "social compacts" which gave structure and purpose to his life — Salomon as an individual with a family, in a personal Jewish community, in the Masonic Order, each with its place in the larger community.

In our age, when people turn to self-help books to learn "networking," revolution is often a form of revenge against isolation and rejection. Such movements seem equal to the task of destroying existing institutions, but not to building something viable in their place. In contrast, Haym Salomon and his contemporaries, immersed as they were in the society they sought to serve, proved themselves successful builders.

Theirs was a unique success. The United States is now entering its third century with its institutions intact. With all its too-evident shortcomings, it is still the best hope of mankind. In studying the people who built the nation, we might gain insight into the ingredients for building a better future. In this regard, the seemingly isolated instances of marriage and betrothal, the giving of charity, dealing with the affairs of the synagogue, which at first seem to have little to do with the making of a two-centuries-old superpower, deserve a place among the grains of history passed on to us. With them we can trace a story of hope and pragmatism which can serve as a link with the past and an ethical reminder of where we yet have to go.

*Arno Penzias*

Arno Penzias shared the 1978 Nobel Prize for Physics. Currently vice president of research at Bell Laboratories, he is a member of the National Academy of Sciences and the Committee of Concerned Scientists.

# Introduction

The great men, one might suppose, are those who are remembered regardless of how they went about their lives and their deeds. Their blemishes are not glaring but, instead, shocking because unexpected. Their acts are quietly immortal because not inscribed with the author's hand trying to both tempt and control fate. This shyness with history creates its own problems. No photograph remains, so every artist creates in his own image rather than the object's true visage. Rumors become myths, translatable into every side of a political or ethnic argument.

This book concerns Haym Salomon and the people he ran across during a time which had its own emotional and psychological fervor. Some of those people are famous even today, but most were the unknowns with an impact upon smaller circles and events which, in totality, create the true bloodstream of society. The "little Jew" represents the type of person who is generally well known, enough so that he achieves the status of a vague question mark throughout history. He was Salomon,

1

Solomon, Solomons. He was Haym and Hayim. He knew wealth and poverty in cycles.

After Salomon died, intestate, his son, Haym M. Salomon, pressed Congress not only to recognize Salomon's contributions to the Revolution but also to repay money Salomon was alleged to have advanced for the cause. From the Twenty-Ninth Congress on, committee reports were submitted which read, in part, "Haym Salomon contributed largely of his pecuniary means toward carrying on the war of the Revolution, aiding the public treasury by frequent loans of moneys and advancing liberally of his means to sustain many of the public men engaged in the struggle for independence ... From the evidence in possession of this Committee, the patriotic devotion of Haym Salomon to the cause of American independence cannot, in their judgment, be questioned ... The committee ... are induced to consider Haym Salomon as one of the truest and most efficient friends of the country in a very critical period of its history ... He seems to have trusted implicitly to the national honor ..."

As Broker to the Office of Finance, Salomon had to cope with those financial complexities inherent in the volatile birth of nations. Loans were often in the form of bills of exchange, which were pieces of paper given a monetary value backed by a national government. They were as good as specie, or money coined from gold and silver. The bill was signed by the seller and given to the purchaser for the latter's note—a contract setting a time limit and interest level. When the note fell due, it had to be honored in the equivalent of specie. There were also Morris notes, drawn up by Morris and backed by him and the government based on bills of exchange. Then there was the matter of government certificates, currencies, taxation, trade contracts with foreign countries, and so on. Salomon had to know what bills were expected, because flooding the market would lower the price. Similarly, he had to observe the activities of merchants, because losses from the British blockade would lower the price. The Bank of North America had to be watched since it discounted notes, that is; accepted them as a basis for specie, bills or loans according to market levels.

Many records concerning Salomon were destroyed when Washington was burned down in 1814. The main sources of documentation are his letters, his signature on bills of exchange and notes, court documents, and newspapers. These are, in any event, enough to sketch a life that has always been a source of dispute.

# I. The Revolution Begins

It was 1776, a restless time when people still wondered whether skirmishes and taxes might not be forgiven and a final break with Britain averted. Congress had previously recommended that the colonies form their own governments. Then, on June 7, the Virginia delegate Richard Henry Lee proposed "that these United Colonies are, and of right ought to be, free and independent States." The resolution was seconded by John Adams and opened to debate.

That same month, in New York City, Haym Salomon approached Leonard Gansevoort. Salomon was a Jewish merchant and a Whig.[1] He wanted "to go suttling to Lake George." A sutler was a merchant who sold provisions to soldiers.

Salomon's birth is traditionally placed in Lissa, Poland, sometime around 1740. The only factual basis for selecting Lissa is that later in his life Salomon addressed letters to his parents there, but it serves, if not accurately, as an imaginative probability of Salomon's underpinnings.

Lissa was a microcosm of flights and returns mirroring the

general history of Jewish wanderings. Jews had been expelled from England in 1290, from France in 1306, from Spain and Portugal in the late fifteenth century. Jews were not only expelled from Germany during the Black Death of 1348–49, but were also blamed for causing the holocaust in the first place. It was those Jews who had wandered into Poland at the invitation of Casimir III the Great.

Lissa, or Polnisch Lissa or Leszno, was incorporated in 1534. In the southwest of Poland, it was near Poznan (Posen), Wroclaw (Breslau), Legnica (Liegnitz) and Lubin. Jews, mainly Germanic, settled in the northern part of the town under authorization of Count Andreas Lescynski. By 1626, there were a synagogue and cemetery. The community was based on the kahal, a council of rabbis which kept spiritual and economic order. In agreement with the Polish government, the kahal collected taxes from the Jews and beth-din, or Jewish court, composed of rabbis and elders. Each community also tried to have a house of prayer, mikve (purifying bath) and cemetery. If any element was lacking, facilities were shared with other communities. The Council of the Four Lands was the central spiritual and social organ for the nation's Jews.

The synagogue burned down in 1656. Three years later, the town's populace fled from Swedish invasion forces. Then the Russians invaded during the Northern War of 1706–07, burning down the rebuilt synagogue, pillaging the community and leaving behind a plague that was blamed on the returning Jews. They were expelled. They returned. They built another temple.

After the Swedish invasion, the Council of the Four Lands (which oversaw all the Jewish communities in Poland) had proclaimed: "Gravely have we sinned before the Lord. The unrest grows from day to day . . . Our people has no standing whatsoever among the nations."[2] This isolation served to perpetuate both the stability of tradition and the anomie of rebellion in its different forms. Periodically, messianic movements swept across eastern Poland. The first had been Molko, a marrano[3] converted to Judaism by the gnome Reuveni. More successful was Sabbatai Zevi, who believed in fasting, bathing in ice-holes and divesting oneself of property. He later converted to Islam when his march to the Promised Land was interrupted by the Sultan of Turkey. His avatar, Jacob Franks — whose real name was Leibowicz — preached a "higher Torah" of God, Messiah, Shekhinah and mass orgies. That led to Talmud burnings in Podolia and the conversion of Frankists to Christianity.

Poland stagnated in the 1700s, and by 1760, Alexander Josef v. Sulkowski, who controlled Lissa, had to grant his Jewish community a four-year hiatus in the collection of taxes. But each year added more interest to the principal indebtedness.[4] In 1764, the General Confederacy met and drew up a constitution which effectively undermined the Council of the Four Lands by directly taxing Jews (two guldens per Jew). A registration drive was begun.

Salomon probably left Poland during that time period, although tradition has it that he migrated in 1772 because of the Partition. Yet it was more common for males from large families to leave during an economic decline, for the sake of easing the burden on their family; they set out to make a living for themselves and, later, to be able to send some money home. Lissa was not overly affected by the Partition, especially when compared to eastern Poland.

There is one other item which supports that time period. On July 10, 1764, a Hyam Solomons signed a voucher in the receipt book of Judah and Moses M. Hays, New York merchants.[5] The likelihood of that being Salomon is extremely strong. Unfortunately, ship records of immigrants during the 1760s are scant, and so from where and when Salomon arrived can never be exactly known.

Salomon, like other wandering Jews, had fled instability earmarked for Jews and found his middle age in a land verging on total collapse of its political and commercial structure. Not that many Jews ever ventured to America from the time of its discovery through the eighteenth century. By 1790, there were perhaps 3,000 Jews out of a population of 3,900,000. Moreover, America was not known as being tolerant. The early Jewish settlers had had to force themselves into the community of New Amsterdam, and during the ensuing years the question of leading "the Indians and other blind people to the knowledge of God" had become a violent undercurrent. One example of the difficulty Jews experienced surfaced during the 1764 campaign for the Pennsylvania General Assembly. Benjamin Franklin's party published an article attacking Jews in the hope of getting Philadelphia's German vote. They barely lost the election.

In medieval Europe, societal integration for the Jew was ultimately a choice between conversion or death. The grey line was those who "converted" yet retained Judaism in secret. Later, during the Aufklärung, the choice broadened into a philosophical projection of all races living together as social equals sometime in the future. The Jewish reaction was two-sided: assimilationists and Salon Juden on the one hand (i.e., rebels), and those who were for continuing racial isolation on the other. This latter was seen not just as a necessity for preserving traditional Jewish values, but also as the impetus for eventually resettling in the Promised Land. "And the ransomed of the LORD shall return, and come to Zion with singing; everlasting joy shall be upon their heads; they shall obtain joy and gladness, and sorrow and sighing shall flee away." (Isaiah 35:10.)[6]

Salomon fought for religious tolerance in Pennsylvania later in his life. And perhaps that is the clue to explaining his devotion to the Revolution. The war was being fought on two different levels: the economic and the ideal. It was obvious that England was draining the colonies through continued taxation aimed at shoring up Britain's credit after the Seven Years War; further, Britain looked upon the colonies as a British marketplace. The Revolution was also being fought on the basis of a social compact, an actual allegiance between man and State. The ideal was a stability between man and government drawn from certain rights which could not be taken away.

Later events will show Salomon to have been extremely moralistic, not just in his support of the Revolution at a time when most Americans cared little about major political upheavals, and his interest-free "loans" to certain figures of the Revolution, but also in his support of Judaism as a traditional creed. He was not an "educated" man, yet his views show how he adhered to the commandments of the Pentateuch.[7]

Thus his desire to "go suttling" in a lake in upper New York State. Troops were stationed in Fort Ticonderoga, under the command of General Arthur St. Clair and Major-General Philip Schuyler. Gansevoort wrote to Schuyler on the twelfth, stating Salomon's request and adding, that Salomon had "hitherto sustained the character of being warmly attached to America."

After his journey, Salomon returned to an altered city. The streets of New York were barricaded and, walking along the docks of the East River, one could vaguely hear soldiers digging embankments on Brooklyn Heights. There was a sense of expectation, a waiting for the slapping of water against the piers to break into explosions of cannon and Tory cheers. No one believed that Washington could hold off the British assault. He had nine thousand men on the Heights, commanded by Putnam, and another nine thousand grouped in Long Island and Manhattan. The British general, Howe, and his subordinate, Sir Henry Clinton, were approaching with over twenty thousand soldiers.

*The New-York Gazette*

Monday December 16, 1765

> The Land was double-tax'd, we thought,
>     To carry on the War:
> The War is to a period brought,
>     But Taxes as they were —
> Strange conduct this! all must allow. —
>     Hush! let your murmurs cease:
> The Land is double-taxed now,
>     To carry on the Peace.

\*

*British Trade to the Colonies*[8]

| *1704* | *Pounds, Sterling* |
|---|---|
| Exports to North America and the West-Indies | £485,265 |
| Exports to Africa | 86,665 |
| | Total £571,930 |

| *1772* | |
|---|---|
| Exports to North America and the West-Indies | £4,791,734 |
| Exports to Africa | 866,398 |
| Export trade to and from Scotland | 364,000 |
| | Total £6.022,132 |

A more startling comparison is that in 1704, total British exports worldwide were valued at £6,509,000. By 1772, British exports to only the American colonies almost equaled that figure.

The synagogue in Mill Street was being closed down. Ger-
shom Mendes Seixas, the hazan, warned the congregation to
flee. Some of Shearith Israel's members—Samuel Judah,
Hayman Levy, Jacob Moses, Jacob Meyers, Jonas Phillips and
Isaac Seixas—had signed a resolution of nonimportation of
British goods, issued after the Townshend Acts of 1767. Like
Salomon, Levy was also supplying the Continental army. Isaac
Franks, seventeen, was a private in Colonel Lasher's militia,
stationed on Long Island.

Most of the Jews moved to Philadelphia, which was a
larger seaport than New York and the meeting place for the
Continental Congress. On August 22—the day Howe landed
twenty thousand men at Gravesend Bay, Long Island—hazan
Seixas hurried from the city with his family. They went to Strat-
ford, Connecticut, taking with them the temple's "Sepharim and
Chests."

Salomon did not leave. There was as yet silence. Howe
split up his troops. General Grant led the Highland regiments
along the coast road of Long Island. General von Heister and
his Hessians went by Bedford and Flatbush. Howe, Clinton,
Percy, Cornwallis and their men used Jamaica Road. The
British overpowered the Americans in the Battle of Long Island
and advanced on Brooklyn Heights. Washington brought up
another thousand men so that he would have a force of ten thousand when the attack came. But it never did. Howe laid siege
to the Heights, hoping that his fleet could sail to the East River
in time to totally surround Washington. Washington frantically
sent men to find any boats they could, and on the night of
August 29 he had his army ferried across to Manhattan. Two
weeks later, Howe followed, landing his men at Kipp's Bay
(about three miles north of Wall Street). There was a small skirmish. The next day, September 16, there was another skirmish
at Harlem Heights.

The entry of the British affected the remaining Jews in different ways. Isaac Franks was captured near Kipp's Bay and imprisoned. On September 22, a fire broke out along the docks and as it surged up Duke Street, it destroyed many of the houses owned by Hayman Levy. A short time after the occupation was completed, Salomon was arrested as a spy and imprisoned in the Provost.

The Provost was the worst prison on the island. It had been built in 1759 and was commanded by the brutal William Cunningham, a man who was later hanged in England on forgery charges. Cunningham put as many prisoners as he could in each cell, letting them out at times so they could be tortured.

Salomon survived, as he advised a relative later, not because of a Talmudic upbringing, but because he had assimilated certain knowledge necessary for his journey to America. He had learned a number of "Christian" languages while traveling through Europe. The wandering Jew lived because of his wits. As he wrote to the Continental Congress, "[Y]our Memorialist was some time before the Entry of the British Troops at the said City of New York and soon after taken up as a Spy and by General Robertson committed to the Provost — That by Interposition of Lieut. [*sic*] General Heister (who wanted him on account of his knowledge in the French, Polish Russian Italian &c Languages) he was given over to the Hessian Commander who appointed him in the Commissary Way as purveyor chiefly for the Officers . . ." In a society not relaxed with the idea of giving Jews complete freedom or control, Salomon apparently shared his appointment with a Tory merchant, William Tongue, who had an office in Hanover Square.

12

*The New-York Gazette and the Weekly Mercury*

Monday September 30, 1776

A Merchant Broker's Office and
Auction or Public Vendue Room
is opened by William Tongue.
. . . The said William Tongue,
having the supply of his Majesty's
guards, and the Hessian officers . . .

Salomon soon began helping French and American
prisoners to escape.[9] He had a continuing association with a
Monsieur Samuel Demezes, an imprisoned Frenchman who
was important enough to merit almost daily torture at the Provost. And Salomon tried to persuade Hessian officers to resign
their commissions.

In the midst of these dangerous activities, Salomon married Rachel Franks. Moses Benjamin Franks had also remained
in the city. His son was the Isaac Franks who served in Lasher's
regiment, was arrested during the British landing on Manhattan and then escaped a few months later. His daughter was
Rachel, age fifteen. Salomon was thirty-seven. Such arrangements, where the man was much older than the woman, were
common at that time. Abraham I. Abrahams, one of the
spiritual leaders of Congregation Shearith Israel, drew up the
marriage certificate, or ketuba. Vows were exchanged on July
6, 1777, the first of Tammuz, 5537.[10]

Since there were so few Jews, proportionately, in America,
and since Jewish families tended to be large, marriage often
acted as much more than a social bond. The prestigious Franks
family exemplified that principle while at the same time reveal-
ing those stresses that affected American Jews as a whole. Jacob
Franks, born in Germany in 1688, went to London, then New
York, where he established himself as a merchant. In 1712, he

13

married Bilhah Abigail, the daughter of Moses Levy and his first wife, Rycha. Moses Levy had also been born in Germany, then gone to London and finally New York. Besides Bilhah Abigail, he had three sons with Rycha: Nathan, Isaac and Michael. One of his sons by his second wife, Grace, was Hayman Levy.

The Franks and the Levys had arrived in New York at a time when Jewish life was not yet formally established in the city. The first Jews in the area had come only half a century earlier. Those had been Sephardic Jews from Spain and Portugal. Towards the turn of the sixteenth century, a Portuguese marrano, Fernando de Loronha, had decided it would be safer to sail to the South American wilderness than to remain near the Inquisition. A compact was drawn up with King Manuel the Great, whereby Loronha and his followers would be allowed to go to Brazil if they promised to explore the coast and build forts in the name of Portugal. But Jewish settlements in Brazil were short-lived; by the early 1650s, the Dutch were vying for the same area. The Jews sided with the invaders and, upon losing, fled to New Amsterdam.

That first boat load of twenty-four Jews arrived one month after the ship *Pear Tree (de Pereboom)*, which had landed on August 22, 1654. On board the *Pear Tree* were Jews coming directly from Holland, which had opened itself up to Jews in 1593. New Amsterdam's governor, Peter Stuyvesant, and one of his religious councilors, Dominie Johannes Theodorus Polheymus, could not stand Jews and, besides, the town's regulation stated that colonists "shall practise no other form of divine worship within their territory than that of the Reformed religion." Stuyvesant also feared that, if Jews were given rights, he would have to do the same for "Lutherans and Papists."

To break the deadlock, the Jews petitioned the Dutch West India Company itself. The company immediately dispatched a

"Grant of Privileges"—Jews were to be given their rights because of the losses they had sustained in Brazil and because of the capital the Dutch Jews had invested in the company. In November, 1655, Asser Levy van Swellem and Jacob Barsimson petitioned for the right to guard the town as burghers (citizens) against Indian attack. This was later permitted and Levy, who was probably Moses Levy's grandfather, and who was a butcher located at the east end of Wall Street, ultimately contributed 100 florins towards the rebuilding of the town's defenses.

Then the British conquered the Dutch and the port was renamed New York. Including slaves, there were about 4,000 people living in the city, mainly below Wall Street, which was actually walled as a fortification against attack. The Jews, still mainly Sephardic, formed a congregation which met in the house of John Harpendingh during the early 1700s. Sometime in 1728, a move was made to the house of David Provost, "a frame building on Mill Street in the first ward about one hundred feet east of the lot occupied in 1729."[11] On that lot was built the synagogue. Jacob Franks, who contributed heavily to the building, laid one of the cornerstones.

Mill Street was eventually nicknamed "Jews' alley" by New Yorkers. By 1746, when the population of the city was about 14,000, there were only fifty-one members of the congregation. The rituals were Sephardic and the services conducted in Hebrew, Portuguese and English, even though Ashkenazim— German and East European Jews—were becoming the majority. A hazan, David Mendes Machado, had been hired in 1736. Besides him, there were a parnas (president), two parnassim, an adjunta (board of trustees), a shamas (sexton), a shohet (ritual slaughterer), a bodek (inspector of cattle), a moil and a Hebrew school.

15

*The New-York Gazette*

Monday May 19, 1777

To be LETT
A Large store and stable in Mill-Street
near the Jews Synagogue. Enquire of ELIAS
DESBROSSES.

Monday June 9, 1777

THREE parts of a Store-house to let in
the Jews-alley or Mill-street. . . .

In 1759, Joseph Jessurum Pinto became hazan. Machado had died a few years before. Joseph and his brother Isaac had come to New York from Amsterdam, after a stop in London.[12] That same year, Congregation Shearith Israel contributed £149.0.6 to Congregation Jeshuat Israel in Newport, Rhode Island, so that they could build a synagogue. The Newport Jewry, headed by Rabbi Isaac de Abraham Touro, included Moses and Aaron Lopez, Jacob Rivera, Joseph de Lucena and Naphtali Hart, most of whom worked in the spermaceti candle business. There was a great deal of contact between the two groups. For example, Judah Hays, a New York merchant, also had business interests in Newport. His daughter, Reyna, eventually married Rev. Touro.

Hayman Levy became parnas of Shearith Israel in 1760. It was apparent to everyone that not only was the congregation not growing, there was a trend among Jews towards intermarriage and nonkosher foods. A drive was started to round up unaffiliated Jews, with the result that services could barely be conducted. A constitution was prepared, in effect from 1761 to 1784. Article nine read: "Every person congregating with us is to behave orderly." Article ten was more adamant: "In case of any indecency or disturbance during our Holy Service, The

Parnas or acting Ruler is hereby obliged calmly to admonish the offender and if he; she or they persists ... the Parnassim on the first proper day following ... shall make complaint ... to a Magestrate for redress."[13] Among the signers of the constitution was Jacob Franks.

Jacob had already observed the trend towards assimilation firsthand. His son David, born in 1720, had married Margaret Evans, the daughter of Peter Evans, who was Philadelphia's Registrar of Wills. Their children were baptized. David did not attend services, but he did stay involved in the affairs of the congregation. However much it hurt Jacob, he did not isolate himself from his son. The two worked together as king's agents (contractors) for the British army during the French and Indian War, handling directly and indirectly a total of £750,000 worth of provisions. One person David suttled for was George Washington.

Although he traveled extensively, David considered Philadelphia his home. His close friend and relative was Nathan Levy, Moses' son. Levy had come to Philadelphia in 1737 and a year later applied for a burial plot for his child. Two years after that, he sought more land for a family cemetery at Spruce Street, between Eighth and Ninth Streets. This latter became known as the first Jewish cemetery in Philadelphia.

David and Nathan formed the company Levy and Franks and soon owned numerous ships: *Drake, Sea Flower, Myrtilla, Richa, Phila*. In 1752, Isaac Norris, Speaker of the Pennsylvania Assembly, commissioned Levy and Franks to bring a bell from England. Norris, a scholar, fluent in Hebrew, had worked before with Levy when he was involved in the manufacture and shipping of beer. As for the London side of the firm, arrangements were taken care of by Moses Franks, David's brother. So it was that in August the ship *Myrtilla* delivered what was to be later known as the Liberty Bell.

When the Revolution came, David sided with the British, while two of his nephews, Isaac and David Salisbury, fought in the Continental army. David S., Moses Franks' son, had left London and settled in Montreal, where he was a merchant. In 1775, he was imprisoned as a Whig sympathizer.

After the siege and surrender of St. John's Fort, General Richard Montgomery marched his troops to nearby Montreal and entered the city November 12. David S. promptly gave money and provisions in support of the army and then joined it as a volunteer. During the course of the next year, he journeyed south to Albany and then arrived in Philadelphia at about the same time that his cousin, Rachel, was marrying Haym Salomon in British-occupied New York.

# II. Jews Flee New York

Before the occupation, most New York merchant activities occurred in the Merchant's Coffee-House. With the arrival of the British, a Mrs. Treville opened the London Coffee-House on lower Broad Street, with a seating capacity of fifty Tories. But free trade was restrained somewhat by the British. Lists were published stating how much could be charged for goods and services at public houses. Similarly, those items which were a necessity for the army were controlled outright. Nonetheless, Salomon accumulated a small fortune working as a merchant and commissary agent and was soon able to rent a house, No. 222 Broad Street, near the post office.

*The New-York Journal or The General Advertiser*

Thursday May 14, 1772

The Merchant's Coffee-House, late in the occupation of Mrs. Ferrari, and now of Elizabeth Wragg, on the opposite cross corner to the new House — is now fitted up in a most neat and commodious Manner, for the recep-

tion of Merchants and other Gentlemen, who will please
to favour her with their Company; where may be had
Breakfast every Morning, and Relishes at all Hours —
Coffee as usual &c.

To survive as a merchant, broker or agent meant develop-
ing the ability to manipulate and balance conflicting currencies
and commodities — an ability paralleling Salomon's learning of
"Christian" languages for the purpose of survival. Before the
French and Indian War, colonial legislatures issued fiat money
through land banks. This money was actually a state "loan,"
issued at 5 percent interest in the expectation that the accumulated interest would pay the cost of government. But the
war changed that, forcing the colonies to emit £2,500,000
sterling in currency and certificates based on future tax
revenues. Meanwhile, Britain directly taxed the colonies.

Regardless of how money was raised or spent, there was
the interminable problem of not knowing how much one's
money was worth. The 1704 Proclamation of Queen Anne had
declared £1 sterling equal to $4.44 4/9 American proclamation
money. The assay of this specie — a coin minted from gold or
silver — had been done by Sir Isaac Newton. Unfortunately, the
colonies were issuing specie of different gross weights while
printing a variety of paper monies.

*The Royal Gazette*

Superintendant General's Office

Those Inhabitants of this City,
who want to purchase
F L O U R,
Are desired to leave their Names at
this Office, in Wall-street, every
Tuesday and Friday, at Ten o'Clock
in the Morning.     May 14, 1778

## Jews Flee New York

As the Revolution got under way, the Continental Congress found itself short of money. On June 22, 1775, it passed this resolution: "Resolved, that a sum not exceeding two millions of Spanish milled dollars be emitted by the Congress in bills of credit for the defence of America. That the Twelve Confederated Colonies be pledged for the redemption of the bills ..." The colonies were given temporary tax quotas to fill, based on an approximation of population in each colony, "Negroes and Mulattoes" included.

What actually happened was that Congress began printing money at the rate of about $1.5 million each month. The money immediately depreciated in value. Loan offices were established in the colonies, and in October, 1776, $5,000,000 worth of loan office certificates (government bonds) were issued at 4 percent to 6 percent interest. The bonds were sold in denominations of $200 and up, and few people bought them. Simultaneously, Congress attempted to pay off the army's suppliers with certificates of indebtedness, which also bore interest.

But merchants and farmers wanted hard money. That meant specie or bills of exchange. A bill was like a contemporary check: It represented a sum of money (written in) drawn from a certain bank and issued to a person who could then sell it or use it to buy goods. The banks, however, were located in England, France, Holland, and other countries, making it difficult for the average person to cash the bill for specie. For that reason, the value of a bill often dropped once it reached America.

*The New-York Gazette*

Monday July 22, 1776

Bills of Exchange from £.100, to £.1000, to be sold. Enquire in the Coffee-House, or the Printer hereof.

21

The second series of loan office certificates were issued in February, 1777, and, carried a face value of 6 percent interest, which fluctuated from 7.5 to an astonishing 30 percent. That was because the certificates could be bought at par with Continental currency, which was rapidly depreciating in value, whereas the interest was paid in specie or bills of exchange. Speculators had a heyday, leading to the withdrawal of the 1777 certificates in 1778 with the further caveat that Congress would from thenceforth pay the interest in paper money. The Congressional threat was nothing more than a return to normalcy. During the period of 1775 to 1779, Congress ordered the printing of $160,000,000 worth of paper money. In 1775, $1 in Continental currency was pegged to $1 in specie. By 1779, it was worth .04 percent of $1 in specie.

This crisis led George Clinton, the Governor of New York State, to propose taxation of the states. The New York Assembly even agreed, in a letter dated October 16, 1778: "We entirely agree with your Excellency, that the depreciation of the paper currency, is a circumstance of an alarming nature, and that taxation is the only effectual and rational remedy." What one says on paper in revolutionary fervor is usually no more than an invitation to read between the lines. The more amenable solution was to see if a foreign country would finance the war. As early as June, 1776, Silas Deane had been shipped off to France as commercial and political agent for the United States. That December, Benjamin Franklin and Arthur Lee moved in with him. The triad was called Commissioners Plenipotentiary. By then, Vergennes, the French minister, had already funnelled one million livres and "an equal sum from Spain" through General Beaumarchais, who was in America. On February 6, 1778, treaties of alliance were signed between France and the United States.

*To the Inhabitants:*

Friends and Countrymen — The present situation of Public Affairs demands your most serious Attention, and particularly the great and increasing Depreciation of your Currency requires the immediate, strenuous, and united efforts of all true Friends to their Country, for preventing an extension of the Mischiefs that have already flowed from that Source . . .

For defraying the Expenses of this uncommon War, your Representatives in Congress were obliged to emit Paper Money; an Expedient that you know to have been before generally and successfully practised in this Continent.

They were very sensible of the Inconveniences with which too frequent Emissions would be attended, and endeavored to avoid them. For this Purpose, they established loan-offices so early as in October, 1776, and have, from that time to this, repeatedly and earnestly solicited you to lend them Money on the faith of the United States. The sums received on loan have nevertheless proved inadequate to the public exigencies. Our Enemies prosecuting the War by sea and land with implacable fury and with some success, Taxation at home and Borrowing abroad, in the midst of difficulties and dangers, were alike impracticable. Hence the continued necessity of new Emissions.

But to this cause alone we do not impute the Evil before mentioned. We have too much reason to believe it has been in part owing to the Artifices of men who have hastened to enrich themselves by monopolizing the necessaries of Life, and to the Misconduct of inferior officers employed in the Public Service . . .

Place your several Quotas in the Continental Treasury — Lend money for public uses — Sink the Emissions of your respective States — Prevent the Produce of the country from being monopolized — Effectually Superintend the behavior of Public Officers . . .

John Jay, *President*
*Continental Congress*
*May 26, 1779*

The army suffered most. In September, 1776, to alleviate some of the pain of service, Congress established a schedule of bounty lands: Colonels received 500 acres, Captains 300, non-commissioned officers and privates 100.[1] The soldiers, however, wanted money, as did merchants. The result was low morale, lack of food and ammunition, and a tendency to plunder in the excess. Matters became worse when the French arrived. As James Tilton wrote to Thomas Rodney: "It must be mortifying to our poor devils to observe the comfortable and happy life of French soldiers. They appear on parade every day like fine gentlemen."

*Continental Army*
Budget May, 1776[2]

| | £ | s. | d. | | | |
|---|---|---|---|---|---|---|
| Commander-in-chief | 8 | 0 | 6 | | | |
| Surgeons, secretaries, etc. | 41 | 17 | 0 | | | |
| 60 Regiments: officers and 30,600 privates | 2263 | 10 | 0 | | | |
| Flying Camp: officers and 8,692 privates | 520 | 10 | 0 | | | |
| Jersey Brigade: officers and 2,856 privates | 200 | 6 | 6 | | | |
| Militia, in pay: officers and 2,700 privates | 1892 | 14 | 0 | | | |
| Total | 4926 | 18 | 0 | 4926 | 18 | 0 |

| | £ | s. | d. |
|---|---|---|---|
| Rations on an average 3 per day, for general and other officers, 4,898 at 2s.6d. | 612 | 5 | 0 |

24

|  | £ | s. | d. |  |  |  |
|---|---|---|---|---|---|---|
| Non-commissioned officers and privates, 80,248 at 10d.* | 3343 | 13 | 4 |  |  |  |
| Total | 3955 | 18 | 4 | 3955 | 18 | 4 |
| Clothing, 49,248 at 2d. per day | 410 | 8 | 0 | 410 | 8 | 0 |
| Total, daily expenses (pounds, sterling) |  |  |  | 9295 | 4 | 4 |

Salomon, apparently acting as a broker and sometime merchant, was able to accumulate a few thousand pounds before and after the British occupied the city. A slave, simply named Joe, was purchased. Salomon also began an association with Jewish Hessian soldiers, brought about by an incident of vandalism. When the British first entered the city, they took over all the churches — except those belonging to Episcopalians, Moravians and Methodists — for use as storehouses and barracks. The locked synagogue was broken into by two British soldiers, who destroyed scrolls and stole silver bells. In protest, the remaining Jews, presumably including Salomon, requested that the temple not be used by the British. The two soldiers were caught and flogged, and the temple was thereafter left untouched. This meant that it could be opened intermittently for services, which were attended by both New York Jews and those Hessian officers who were Jewish.

The war reports in the biased *Royal Gazette* pictured the

---

*Rations costing 10d. per day were to include: 1 lb. fresh beef or salt fish; ¾ lb. pork or 20 oz. salt beef; 1 lb. bread, flour, 1 pint milk, 1 quart cider or spruce beer, per diem each; 3 lb. candles, 8 lb. hard soap, per week for 100 men; 3 pints pease, 1 pint Indian meal, 6 oz. butter, per man per week.

Continental army as demoralized and near defeat. Newport, Rhode Island, had been taken. At the time of their marriage, Haym and Rachel could have looked out any window and seen troops marching towards the fleet docked at the mouth of the East River. Howe quickly shipped his men south to Chesapeake. From there, they marched up through Brandywine and Germantown, rolling aside opposition. Congress fled to Lancaster, and two weeks later, September 26, Cornwallis entered Philadelphia. Less noted were the northern campaigns. Burgoyne's forces had surged out of Canada, surrounding Ticonderoga and driving out General Arthur St. Clair. But then Burgoyne stumbled at the battles of Saratoga (September 19 and October 7, 1777). He surrendered on October 17.

For Salomon, news of Newport and Philadelphia would have immediately brought to mind the congregations already in those cities and those friends of his who had fled New York to seek safety from the British. Clinton was sending messages in the newspapers: You, American soliders, we are of the same blood and motherland, join our side. It was reminiscent somehow, in an inverted sense, of what Pope Innocent III had declared at the Fourth Lateran Council of 1215: Jews were to wear yellow badges from then on.

In this confusion of time and circumstance, Salomon was known as Salomon, Solomon, Hayim, Hayman, Haym. In his first advertisement, his name was Haym Solomons.

*The New-York Gazette*

January 12, 1778 and
January 19, 1778

Ship Bread *and* Fresh Rice,
To be SOLD by
HAYM SOLOMONS,
In Broad-street, No. 222, near the Post-office.

A son, Ezekiel, was born to Haym and Rachel on July 20 and was circumcised eight days later by the moil Abraham I. Abrahams, who noted in his "Registry of Circumcisions":

> 79. On Tuesday July 28 1778      4 Ab 5538
>      Haym Solmss. son                Ezekiel son of Hayim
>      Ezekiell in N York

The boisterous Howe had been recalled to Britain having proved himself more of a party-goer than a commander in war. Sir Henry Clinton replaced him as chief commander. Philadelphia had been evacuated.

On August 5, in New York, as reported in *The Royal Gazette*, "On Monday Morning about one o'clock the city was alarmed by a tremendous fire, which broke out at the House of Mr. Stewart, at Cruger's dock." The flames spread along Little Dock Street, consuming sixty-four houses, two small vessels and some stores. Colonel Cockburn's 35th Regiment tried putting the fire out. Suddenly, a flash of lightning struck a magazine of powder aboard the sloop *Morning Star*, and neighboring roofs and windows were shattered.

Less than a week later, this confluence of events spilled over into Salomon's life and he had to flee the city, taking Joe with him. In his memorial to the Continental Congress, he wrote that "he [Salomon] has been of great Service to the French and American prisoners . . . That this and his close connexions with such of the Hessian Officers as were inclined to resign and with Monsieur Samuel Demezes has rendered him at last so obnoxious to the British Head Quarters that he was already pursued by the Guards and on Tuesday the 11th inst, he made his happy Escape from thence." His escape, if happy, nonetheless left behind his family and his fortune, the latter irretrievably lost, the former perhaps so. This, indeed, is trust, or faith. "Behold, happy is the man whom God reproves . . . In famine he will redeem you from death, and in war from the power of the sword." (Job 5:17,20.) Luzatto, in *Mesillat Yesharim*, would have added, "The test of this love is during a time of hardship and trouble ... 'Whatever Heaven does is for the best.' This means that even hardship and trouble are apparent evils which in reality are good."[3]

### To the Honorable the Continental Congress

The Memorial of Hyman Solomon late of the City of New York, Merchant. Humbly Sheweth,

That your Memorialist was some time before the Entry of the British Troops at the said City of New York and soon after taken up as a Spy and by General Robertson committed to the Provost—That by Interposition of Lieut. General Heister (who wanted him on account of his knowledge in the French, Polish Russian Italian &c Languages) he was given over to the Hessian Commander who appointed him in the Commissary Way as purveyor chiefly for the Officers—That being at New York he has been of great Service to the French and American prisoners and has assisted them with Money and helped them off to make their Escape—That this and his close connexions with such of the Hessian Officers as were inclined to resign and with Monsieur Samuel Demezes has rendered him at last so obnoxious to the British Head Quarters that he was already pursued by the Guards and on Tuesday the 11th inst, he made his happy Escape from thence—This Monsieur Demezes is now most barbarously treated at the Provost's and is seemingly in danger of his life. And the Memorialist begs leave to cause him to be remembered to Congress for an Exchange.

Your Memorialist has upon this Event most irrevocably lost all his Effects and Credits to the amount of Five or six thousand Pounds Sterling and left his distressed Wife and a Child of a Month old at New York waiting that they may soon have an Opportunity to come from thence with empty hands.

In these Circumstances he most humbly prayeth to

grant him any Employ in the way of his Business whereby he may be enabled to support himself and his family — And your Memorialist as in duty bound &c &c

HAYM SALOMON

Philad.<sup>al</sup> *Aug* 25th 1778

Tradition has it that Salomon was responsible for both the 1776 and the 1778 fires. The dates fit neatly with his initial arrest and eventual flight. But the first fire destroyed the houses owned by Hayman Levy, Salomon's relative. The second fire was believed by the British to have been started by natural causes until Major General Jones, the commander of the forces in New York City, was persuaded otherwise by those who see perpetrators everywhere. On August 14, he issued this proclamation: "Whereas, many inhabitants of this city, suspect that the late fire was not in the effect of accident, but design," a reward of 100 guineas was offered for information. "It is reported that a man suspected to have been concerned, being pursued, was wounded in the back with a bayonet, immediately after the fire broke out." Ships were ordered to remain anchored at a distance from the docks. Slaves, of course, had already attempted to burn down the city, once in 1712 and again during the Great Negro Plot of 1741, during which the homes and warehouses of Captain Warren, Mr. Van Zant, Vergereau and Quick burned to the chantings of "Fire, Fire, Scorch, Scorch, A Little, damn it, By and By!!" But the Continental Congress did not follow suit until its resolution of October 21, 1778: "*Resolved*, that, immediately, when the enemy begin to burn or destroy any town, it be recommended to the good people of these states to set fire to, ravage, burn, and destroy, the houses and properties of all tories."

If Salomon left New York burning, he arrived in a Philadelphia already scorched by occupation. Trees and fences

By MAJOR GENERAL JONES,
Commanding in New-York.
## PROCLAMATION.

WHEREAS, many inhabitants of this city, fuspect that the late fire was not the effect of accident, but defign. Any perfon, or perfons, that will difcover to Major General JONES, one, or more of the Incendiaries, or thofe aiding in fo horrid a crime, fo that he, or they may be brought to juftice, fhall receive a reward of ONE HUNDRED GUINEAS, on the conviction of fuch offender, or offenders. And as a further encouragement to bring this guilt to light, if the informer has been an accomplice, His Excellency the COMMANDER in CHIEF is pleafed to promife a pardon to the informer, on the conviction of fuch offender, or offenders, befides the above reward of ONE HUNDRED GUINEAS.

It is reported that a man fufpected to have been concerned, being purfued, was wounded in the back with a bayonnet, immediately after the fire broke out.

Given, under my Hand at New-York, this 14th day of Auguft, 1778.

DANIEL JONES.

By Order of the General,
NATHANIEL PHILIPS, Sec'ry

---

New-York, Auguft 3, 1778.

SEveral ftores of various forts being carried on board veffels lying near the whaifs, and alfo to feveral houfes, during the confufion occafioned by the fire. All perfons in poffeffion of fuch ftores, are immediately to give notice to the Mayor, of their quality and quantity. Any perfon concealing fuch effects will be punifhed with the utmoft feverity.

By order of Maj. Gen. JONES.
CHA. ROOKE, Aid de Camp.

"The Royal Gazette," Wednesday, August 19, 1778.

30

had been chopped down for firewood. Houses and churches had been burned and desecrated. Many ex-New York Jews had joined with Philadelphia and Southern Jews in the militia and regiments: Myer Myers, Ephraim Hart, Solomon Simson, Ephraim Abraham, Abraham M. Seixas, Mordecai Sheftall and son, Benjamin Jacobs, Abraham Judah, Moses Judah, Samuel Judah, Hayman Levy, Simon Nathan, Joseph Nathans, Jonas Phillips, the Cardozo's, Aaron and Abraham Isaacs, Hart Jacobs, Solomon Marache. Captain Lushington's "Jew Company," in which Philadelphia's Jacob I. Cohen and Solomon Aaron were privates, would later fight in the South Carolina campaign against Cornwallis.

Salomon, however, applied for his commission from the Congress. But Congress was, as usual, more concerned with finances. Under pressing circumstances, Salomon decided to offer his services as a broker to the French.

# III. Salomon as Broker

The acknowledged means of making money during the Revolution was to speculate in privateering or profiteering. The former meant raiding British vessels with letters of Marque and Reprisal in hand (these were on file with the Court of Admiralty). The latter involved selling tobacco or flour in the West Indies for a large profit and returning to America with other goods to be resold for a higher profit. Isaac Moses, a leader in Philadelphia's Congregation Mickveh Israel, had assets of £115,200 Pennsylvania currency in 1780, was distantly related to Salomon (Reyna, Moses' wife, was a daughter of Hayman Levy), and had interests in eight privateering ships along with Robert Morris (the soon-to-be superintendent of finance), Hayman Levy, Matthew Clarkson (later to be mayor of Philadelphia), Benjamin Seixas (also related to Moses and Salomon through his wife, Zipporah, another daughter of Hayman Levy; his brother, Gershom Mendes Seixas, was the hazan), and Solomon Marache.

Salomon later invested in one such venture for the sake of

building a temple, with disastrous results (as will be discussed in Chapter IV). For now, needing a quick and safe manner of accumulating money so that he could establish himself in Philadelphia and bring his family from New York, Salomon approached Chevalier de La Luzerne for a position.

Luzerne had been born in Paris in 1741. His mother was the well-known, now forgotten writer Malesherbes. Luzerne had served as aide-de-camp to Duke de Broglie, a family relation, and then had become colonel of the Grenadiers. At age thirty-five, he entered the diplomatic corps and served as ambassador to the electorate of Bavaria. When Monsieur Gerard, the minister to America, fell sick, Luzerne was selected as the replacement. The Journals of Congress for Wednesday, November 17, 1779, stated: "According to order, the Honorable Chevalier de La Luzerne, minister plenipotentiary of his Most Christian Majesty, was introduced to the audience by Mr. Matthews and Mr. Morris, the two members for that purpose appointed." The president of Congress, Samuel Huntington, welcomed him. The Chevalier's remarks were translated by Rev. Robert Molyneux, Jesuit rector of St. Mary's Church in Philadelphia, and an English teacher on the side.

Salomon was duly appointed broker to the French consulate and broker to the office of the paymaster-general, both at minimal commissions.[1] Nonetheless, by November, 1780, he had saved £1,200.

*Philadelphia Tax List 1780*[2]

A tax "on Estates and real and Personal" passed by the General Assembly "for funding and redeeming the Bills of Credit of the United States of America and for providing Means to bring the present War to a happy conclusion."
Passed, June 1, 1780     Assessed, November 24, 1780

# Salomon as Broker

| Name | Valuation | Tax | | |
|------|-----------|-----|---|---|
| John Chaloner, merch't | 61,000 | 169 | .8 | .0 |
| Tench Francis, merchant | 186,600 | 513 | .3 | .0 |
| Samuel Inglis & Co. | 13,300 | 33 | .5 | .0 |
| for Th's Willing's estate | 400,000 | 1,000 | .0 | .0 |
| Thomas Fitzgerald, carter | 17,300 | 43 | .5 | .0 |
| Robert Morris, merchant | 80,000 | 200 | .0 | .0 |
| Samuel Inglis, merchant | 50,700 | 126 | .15 | .0 |
| John Ross, merchant | 24,000 | 60 | .0 | .0 |
| Michael Gratz, merchant | 44,800 | 112 | .0 | .0 |
| William Bingham, merchant | 88,900 | 222 | .5 | .0 |
| John Finlay, merchant | 163,400 | 490 | .4 | .0 |
| Thomas Willing, Esq'r | 242,400 | 484 | .16 | .0 |
| Thomas Fitzsimmons | 5,000 | 10 | .0 | .0 |
| Moses Nathan, merch't | 39,400 | 128 | .1 | .0 |
| Jonas Philips, merch't | 49,500 | 160 | .17 | .0 |
| Sampson Levy | 30,800 | 80 | .17 | .0 |
| Samson Levy's est'e | 17,000 | 51 | .0 | .0 |
| Edward Shippen's est'e | 6,000 | 18 | .0 | .0 |
| Michael Gratz, merch't | 47,400 | 165 | .18 | .0 |
| Jacob Frank | 22,000 | 60 | .10 | .0 |
| Moses Mordecai, broker | 7,700 | 23 | .2 | .0 |
| Moses Nathan, merch't, stables | 3,300 | 39 | .18 | .0 |
| James Wilson | 46,500 | 139 | .10 | .0 |
| Jacob Hart, tobacconist | 6,000 | 9 | .0 | .0 |
| Benjamin Sexius | 33,200 | 39 | .12 | .0 |
| Sexius & Levy | 4,000 | 12 | .0 | .0 |
| John Holker, Esq'r | 90,000 | 315 | .0 | .0 |
| Solomon Myers Cohen, merch't | 30,000 | 84 | .0 | .0 |
| Hyman Levy, gentle'n | 11,400 | 39 | .18 | .0 |
| Isaac Moses, merch't | 115,200 | 403 | .4 | .0 |
| Hyman Solomon | 1,200 | 3 | .12 | .2 |

Salomon's newfound prosperity also brought him back his family, which suggests that he had to pay for their safe passage. Rachel gave birth to Deborah. The slave Joe ran away.

*The Pennsylvania Packet*

Saturday November 18, 1780

Philadelphia, November 8, 1780

Six Hundred Dollars Reward.
RAN AWAY from the subscriber, on the 7th inst. a
Negroe MAN named JOE, about 27 years of age, about
5 feet 6 inches high, of a thin stature and pale complexion; had on a brown fustian coat, waistcoat and overalls
of the same, and took sundry other cloaths with him. It
is supposed he will endeavour to pass as a free man, and
make his way to New-York. Whoever takes up said
Negroe, and delivers him to the subscriber, living in
Front-street, three doors above Arbuckle's row, or
secures him in any gaol in the continent, shall have the
above reward and all reasonable charges paid, by
HAYM SOLOMON.
N.B. All masters of vessels and others, are forbid to
harbour or carry him off at their peril.

Salomon offered $600, or approximately $6 specie, for the
return of Joe, which could only be considered cheap, since
rewards for adult slaves ranged from $8 to $50 specie. Appren-
tices were worth 18 pence to ten dollars. Slaves were a com-
modity. Willing and Morris, in an advertisement placed in the
*Pennsylvania Journal and Weekly Advertiser* of June 27, 1765, sold
slaves and empty bottles in the same sentence. Rivera and
Lopez, members of both the New York and Newport congregations, traded in flour, spermaceti candles, and Africans suitable
for sale in Jamaica.

If there is any analogy, Jews had served as indentured ser-
vants. Jonas Phillips, for example, son of the Prussian Aaron
Uriah Faibush, was indentured to Moses Lindo in 1756 in
South Carolina. When freed of his bond, he moved to Albany,
New York, and worked as a trader. He became a master mason
and married Rebecca, daughter of the late hazan David

Mendes Machado. From 1765 to 1770, he was shohet and bodek (slaughterer and examiner of meat) for Congregation Shearith Israel in New York. When he moved to Philadelphia, he opened up a merchant's office near Dunlap's Printing Office on Market Street. By late 1780, Phillips had assets of £49,500 — and two slaves.

In any event, the magnates had slaves, and their companies imported them. In Philadelphia, John Nixon had 2 slaves; Samuel Ingles 1; John Chaloner 1; Edward Shippen 2; Andrew Hamilton 2; Tench Francis 2; James Wilson 3; Robert Morris 1; John Swanwick 3; and Isaac Moses 1. After the Revolution, the Jews were among the first to free slaves *en masse*.

One of those slaveowners, Robert Morris, was described as a "large man with a large head." He was born in Liverpool, England, in 1733. His father was a merchant whose business was trade with the colonies, which led the family to move to Philadelphia in the 1740s. Robert clerked in the firm of Charles Willing, spending most of his time with the son, Thomas Willing, who was known as "Old Square Toes." After the death of the two fathers, they formed Willing & Morris.

What brought Morris and Salomon together was the financial morass. As John Adams wrote Congress from Paris: "The art of war is so well and so equally understood by the great nations of Europe, and they are so equally furnished with Statesmen, Generals, Admirals and other officers, capable of conducting it well, that it is now generally considered as a contest of finances; so that the nation which can longest find money to carry on the war, can generally hold out the longest."

On September 3, 1779, Congress resolved to issue no more than $200,000,000 total in paper currency. By March 18, 1780, that ceiling was reached. Congress therefore took the step of devaluating the currency forty-to-one, to specie. Further, the states were told that for every $40 of paper brought in as

Philadelphia, November 8, 1780.

# Six Hundred Dollars Reward.

RAN-AWAY from the subscriber, on the 7th inst. a Negroe MAN named JOE, about 27 years of age, about 5 feet 6 inches high, of a thin stature and pale complexion; had on a brown fustian coat, waistcoat and overalls of the same, and took sundry other cloaths with him. It is supposed he will endeavour to pass as a freeman, and make his way to New-York. Whoever takes up said Negroe, and delivers him to the subscriber, living in Front-street, three doors above Arbuckle's row, or secures him in any gaol on the continent, shall have the above reward and all reasonable charges paid, by HAYM SOLOMON.

N. B. All masters of vessels and others are forbid to harbour or carry him off at their peril.

payment of taxes, $2 in new bills would be issued at 5 percent interest, payable also in bills. And on June 11, Elbridge Gerry wrote to Robert Morris: "The present reduced State of ye Army & ye Wants of every Species of Supplies ... may all be traced to an exhausted Treasury ... What I mean to propose is an immediate association of ye Merchants ... to support ye late Plan of Congress relative to Finance ... to send unto ye respective loan offices, all ye old Continental Bills of Credit, & receive ye Amount thereof in new Bills at ye Exchange established by ye Resolution of Congress ... every Dollar so exchanged will furnish another for ... ye Army."

Morris, however, did not exactly want to do that; he wanted a temporary bank which would buy supplies for the army. On June 17, the bank was born at the City Tavern in what Morris called "nothing more than a patriotic subscription of Continental money ... for the purpose of purchasing provisions for a starving army." Morris put up £10,000; James Wilson, £5,000; Michael Hillegas, £4,000; Thomas Mifflin, £5,000; Thomas Willing, £5,000; Isaac Moses, £3,000; and so on. Morris badgered Congress until it recognized the Pennsylvania Bank and deposited £15,000 in bills of exchange. Pledges totalled £315,000 by the time the bank opened on July 17. Its office was on Front Street, two doors above Walnut; business hours were 9 to 12 and 3 to 5. It issued notes at 6 percent interest. Not too surprisingly, Morris was chairman of the board of inspectors until the bank closed up shop two months later.

If Morris' basic motivation (as he protested) was not self-interest, he firmly believed everyone else was infected with it to the core. In 1769, after he had married Mary White, he promptly liquidated her land inheritance for $15,860, and reinvested it. He expanded the holdings of Willing and Morris so that by

**Opposite: Salomon's runaway slave notice, "Pennsylvania Packet," Saturday, November 18, 1780.**

39

early 1775, it was free of encumbrances and had extensive investments in trade and real estate. That same year, he became vice president of the Pennsylvania Committee of Safety, a delegate to the Continental Congress and a member of Congress' Secret Commerce Committee, which was responsible for giving out supply contracts. The firm which handled most of the committee's business was Willing and Morris. Between 1775 and 1777, the firm Willing and Morris received $2,483,000 in government contracts. Morris and John Ross, also a wealthy Philadelphia merchant, earned an additional $90,000.

Morris, protestations of honesty aside, was constantly pursued by allegations of overcharging. For example, Arthur Lee, one of the commissioners to France, claimed that Morris often submitted vouchers for goods which were never delivered. Morris responded to Lee's colleague, Silas Deane: "I shall continue to discharge my duty faithfully to the Public, and pursue my Private Fortune by all such honorable and fair means as the times will admit of." Shortly thereafter, Deane was called back from France to defend himself against a charge of mishandling American funds.

Henry Laurens, another Morris-baiter and the South Carolina delegate to Congress, believed that Willing and Morris had exacted payment from Congress for the loss of a ship which was not on government business. There had been the 1776 "Indian Contract," where an $80,000 payment was questioned because there was some doubt that the goods Morris had been paid to ship to Europe were ever sent. There was also the fact that Willing and Morris retained a certain William Bingham as their agent in French Martinique, even if only at half the usual 5 percent commission, and Morris frequently wrote him about the "proffits" to be made from the war.

Yet this delegate, signer of the Declaration of Independence, and profiteer at least moved and did things in an atmosphere of political laziness. As Benjamin Franklin said of Congress' inattention to the financial fiasco which placed such stress on the Continental army, he was shocked to find that most Congressional remittances went "for tea, and a great part of the remainder is ordered to be laid out in gewgaws and superfluities." In contrast, Morris, whether boasting or being sarcastic, wrote to Washington at the turn of the year, 1777: "I am up very early this morning to dispatch a supply of $50,000 to your Excellency . . . but it will not be got away so early as I could wish, for none concerned in this movement, except myself, are up. I shall rouse them immediately."

During the next years, Morris took temporary leaves from Congress so that he could devote himself to his business interests. He privateered with Isaac Moses and William Bingham — one such ship, the *Retaliation*, filled with English rum and sugar, yielded £43,994 to Morris, £29,329 to Bingham, and £14, 664 to Captain Ord. He worked with Peter Whitesides & Co., merchants, and Jonathan Hudson & Co. Hudson, unfortunately, had a penchant for overbuying, and the company's warehouses were quickly stacked with tobacco. Morris, sickened, withdrew. He turned to William Turnball and John Holker. Holker, who speculated successfully in monies, advertised himself as "Agent of the Royal Marine in all the Ports of the United States, Consul of France." Morris put up $200,000 (about $5,000 specie) for William Turnball & Co.

On his own — the firm Willing and Morris had dissolved July 28, 1778 — Morris was selling "brandy, hides, sugars, molasses, rum, pipes, wine" and land in Springfield township. He still contracted for the Secret Commerce Committee, although relations were strained. The committee had begun regulating prices in such a way that working for it was no longer profitable. In July, 1779, Morris complained to Timothy Matlack that his "calculation of a Voyage to St. Eustatia for

Rum Tea or Coffee" would result in a loss of £17,171 18s. unless the committee adjusted its regulations and "lower[ed] the price of Exportable Articles ... in Conformity to the present regulated prices of Imports." Morris' proposal was rejected.

It was perhaps to prove his value and strength in Philadelphia, as opposed to Congress, that Morris formed the Pennsylvania Bank. He brought in his friends James Wilson, Michael Hillegas, Isaac Moses, was himself chairman, and had John Nixon and George Clymer appointed directors. At the same time, he reconciled with Thomas Willing; they bought a wharf together, then added a third partner, Samuel Ingles, whose company had handled the Willing estate. Morris was also planning a commercial house in Nantes, as a venture with James Wilson, the Nesbitts and Silas Deane. Morris' successes prompted more vehement chastisement from Henry Laurens, and some obsequiousness, this from Richard Peters, Secretary of the Board of War, in a letter dated August, 1780: "I am conscious of deserving some share of the advantages of this diabolical war. I have earned it by my labor, and by my losses I have gained a right to demand something from Fortune ... I shall pay court to her through you, and by that if it be *possible and proper* I may have a small share in the Privateer Circle."

*The Pennsylvania Packet*

Saturday March 24, 1781

*Bills of Exchange on France*,
London, Amsterdam and St. Eustatia,
TO BE SOLD
By Haym Solomons, Broker:
He also receives Bills, or any Merchandize to sell on commission, and may be met with at JACOB MIER's in Front-street, next door to Stephen Shewell's, facing Pewter-platter-alley, in the forenoon and afternoon. He will also attend from twelve to two at the Coffee-house. Those gentlemen who shall please to favour him with

their commands, may depend upon the greatest care and
punctuality.

Individual profits aside, these were not good years for the
fledgling government. As Morris wrote in *A Statement of the Accounts of the United States of America During the Administration of the
Superintendant of Finance*, "The treasury was then in arrears more
than two millions and a half of dollars ... Public credit was at
an end." Rochambeau noted that "a third of General
Washington's army mutinied; the league of Pennsylvania put
their general and their officers under arrest, and, led on by a
sergeant, marched up to Philadelphia to demand their pay of
Congress ... It was at this period that bills of exchange on
France were negotiated ... at the exorbinant *[sic]* rate of forty
per cent; and that American paper had fallen nearly a hundred
to one [of specie]."[3]

Nothing worked. Congress tried selling public bills in
Havana, perhaps hoping that that was far enough away for in-
vestors not to have heard of the Revolution, but that plan fell
through because of lack of credit.

Similarly, four years after Congressional adoption, the
states had finally ratified the Articles of Confederation, which
dictated in part that no state could have "conference, agreement, alliance or treaty with any king, prince or state" unless
consented to by Congress. The states nonetheless scrambled to
have their own financial agreements with France. Article VIII
established a common United States treasury for the common
defense; the problem was lack of specie or bills.

Congress finally turned to the man who had spent most of
his time making a fortune from the war. Ironically enough,
those factors of selection were probably the wisest. The true
patriot had more likely than not starved to death years before.
Morris, in accepting the position of superintendent of finance,
told Congress, "I sacrifice much of my interest, my ease, my

domestic tranquility. If I know my own heart, I make these sacrifices with a disinterested view to the service of my country. I am willing to go further, and the United States may command everything I have excepting my integrity; and the loss of *that* would effectually disable me from serving them more."

The other point of view is presented by the president of Congress, Reed, who wrote to General Greene (then battling Cornwallis somewhere in the Carolinas) that Morris "claimed a right of continuing in private trade, of dismissing all continental officers, handling public money at pleasure, with many lesser privileges amounting to little less than an engrossment of all those powers of Congress which had been deemed incommunicable . . . But, the public have received a real benefit from Mr. Morris's exertions. At the same time, those who know him will also acknowledge that he is too much a man of the world to overlook certain private interest which his command of the paper and occasional speculations in that currency will enable him to promote."

A retrospective is given in a letter of Samuel Osgood addressed to John Adams and dated December 7, 1783, in which Osgood states that Morris "judges well in almost all Money matters; He judges generally for himself; and acts with great decision. He has many excellent qualities for a Financier, which however do not comport so well with Republicanism, as Monarchy. Ambitious of becoming the first Man in the United States, he was not so delicate in the Choice of Means, and Men for his Purpose, as [are] indispensably necessary in a free Government."

On the other hand, there was Gouvernor Morris. He was a New Yorker who at an early age lost a leg purportedly due to some sexual misadventure no one has had the decency to report upon. When Robert Morris was up for superintendent, the unrelated Gouvernor wrote to the real governor of New York,

Clinton. "If he accepts the office which Congress against his will conferred on him, I shall hope to see some better mode of raising money . . . and I shall be morally certain of honesty in the expenditure." After appointment, Robert hired Gouvernor as his deputy at the government salary of $1,850 annually, since "greatly to curtail salaries is a false economy, because it brings men into office, who are incapable of the duties, or unworthy of confidence."

Morris never thought small. As soon as he took office, he declared that he wanted a national bank this time. Congress adopted his plan by one vote. George Clymer and John Nixon were appointed officers and opened subscriptions on June 5, 1781. Shares were issued at $400 each, to be paid for in gold or silver. Purchases below $2,000 were cash on delivery. Above that amount, half the sum was to be deposited immediately by the purchaser, the rest paid off over three months. A thousand shares had to be sold before the bank could open.

*The Pennsylvania Packet*

The Office, in this City,
For taking SUBSCRIPTIONS to the
*National Bank,*
FOR THE
United States of America,
Is now opened, at the House of Mr. BENJAMIN
FULLER, in Front-street, below the Draw bridge.
GEORGE CLYMER
JOHN NIXON
Philadelphia, 5<sup>th</sup> June, 1781

Shares were not in demand. Even bills drawn on France were falling in value. Worse, Washington wanted money so that he could attack New York along with Rochambeau's French forces.

That was the situation when Haym Salomon walked up to

Robert Morris' large house and waited for the door to be opened by the slave, James. The house had been originally owned by Richard Penn, but it was Morris who was the first in the New World to install hot-houses and ice-houses. The meeting resulted in a generally productive, although sometimes stormy relationship. Salomon agreed to serve as broker, and Morris agreed to pay him a commission of ½ percent or less.

*Robert Morris' Diary*
June 8, 1781

> I agreed with Mr. Haym Salomon, the Broker who had been employed by the Officers of his Christian Majesty to make sales of their Army and Navy Bills, to assist me in the Sale of the Bills I am to draw for the monies granted as aforesaid, his Brokerage to be settled hereafter, but not to exceed a half per cent.

In late June, Rochambeau joined forces with Washington at Philippsburgh, New York, a small town on the Hudson River a few miles north of Manhattan and Clinton's 12,000 British soldiers. The French and American forces totaled 9,000. The plan was to march around Clinton towards Yorktown to coordinate an attack on Cornwallis. Washington's troops, however, had different ideas about forced marches. Washington wrote Morris: "I entreat you to procure one month's pay in specie for the detachment. Part of these troops have not been paid anything for a long time past, and have on several occasions shown marks of great discontent. The service they are going upon is disagreeable to the Northern regiments: but I make no doubt that a douceur [bribe] of a little hard money would put them in proper temper."

Morris began to put together a little federal reserve empire, using Salomon as his front-man. He needed to inflate the market for French bills so that he could sell his at a premium for specie, which would then be sent to Washington. But brokers, such as John Chaloner, were underselling so as to unload their bills. Salomon, who had moved from Jacob Mier's to a house on Front Street between Market and Arch, dropped by to see Morris on August 8. Morris "informed him that Mr. Chaloner had promised not to sell under six Shillings and desired him to press the Sale of Bills. I desire him to gain information of the persons, the sums, the rates, to call on them and urge them to keep up the price to threaten them to give me intelligence tomorrow morning."

The next day, Morris noted in his diary that Luzerne "does not chuse to risque the Loss of Selling Bills for 50,000 Livres at 5/6. I agree with him to give me Bills to that amount in exchange for a number of small Bills. Gave Salomon order to press a Sale on Credit and explained to him plan of preventing others from selling." Salomon left and, finding that bills would sell only under terms of relaxed credit, did so. He returned in the afternoon. "Salomon informs me that he has sold from sixty to eighty thousand Livres at 6/ on a credit of eight months. I refuse and direct it at four months payable part in Hand the remainder monthly." There were few sales. Morris again tried getting other brokers to stop underselling and Salomon, meanwhile, concentrated on state currency.

A week later, August 17, Morris noted that Salomon, "the Jew Broker," had "sold small sums of the Pennsylvania State papers at two dollars for 1 of silver and that he offered to purchase said paper at 2½ for one agreeable to orders I had before given him, and I think it best to continue my orders on this footing until the collection of Taxes Commences. He informs me that Bills of Exchange continue to pour in our market from the Eastern States and other places where the French Bills of 30 days' sight on France are now selling at D/6 to D/9 for five Livres."

*The Pennsylvania Packet*

July 14, 21, 26; August 14, 23, 1781

> *Haym Solomons, Broker,* sells Bills on Holland, France, Spain, England, St. Croix, &c. He likewise sells, on commission, Loan-office Certificates, and all other Kinds of Merchandize. He gives constant attendance at his Office in Front-street, between Market and Arch-streets, from 9 to 12 in the forenoon; likewise attends at the Coffee-house from 12 to 2.

August 23, 28; September 4, 15, 20, 25;
October 2, 6, 9, 13, 1781

> *Haym Salomon, Broker,* At his office in Front-street, between Market and Arch-streets,
> TRANSACTS all kinds of business on Commission. Buys and sells Bills of Exchange on any part of Europe. As also,
> Pennsylvania and other
> State Money,
> And which he receives in payment for
> Bills of Exchange,
> At the highest price given.
> He gives constant attendance at his Office, from nine to one in the forenoon; and from three to seven in the afternoon.

Morris left to confer with Washington. Salomon approached Gouvernor Morris and explained that he wished to undersell some bills so as to unload them in the flooded market. Further, the sales would be on credit. Morris gave his approval and, with that, Salomon tried getting rid of as many bills as he could at four shillings each, as opposed to the other Morris' instructed level of six shillings per. Gouvernor was enraged. "I am much surprised at the information you gave me this morning of the sale of bills on such lax credit. Before you ventured in anything of that sort you should have given me notice of it.

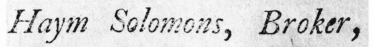

# *Haym Solomons, Broker,*

Sells Bills on Holland, France, Spain, England, St. Croix, &c.

HE likewise sells, on commiffion, Loan-office Certificates, and all other Kinds of Merchandize. He gives conftant attendance at his Office in Front-ftreet, between Market and Arch-ftreets, from 9 to 12 in the forenoon; likewise attends at the Coffee-houfe from 12 to 2.

# *Haym Salomon, Broker,*

At his office in Front-ftreet, between Market and Arch-ftreets,

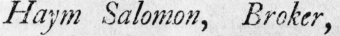

TRANSACTS all kinds of bufinefs on Commiffion. Buys and fells Bills of Exchange on any part of Europe. As alfo,

## Pennfylvania and other State Money,

And which he receives in payment for

## Bills of Exchange,

At the higheft price given.

He gives conftant attendance at his Office, from nine to one in the forenoon; and from three to feven in the afternoon.

"Pennsylvania Packet," Thursday, August 23, 1781.

Though I permitted a certain sum to be sold on credit, I had no idea of any thing of that sort being carried to such an extent. However as you have done it I will not falsify your promise but in future you must not sell on credit at all, nor under six shillings for cash. I will write to Mr. Morris and should he think proper the directions may be altered but not otherwise. I must insist upon an account immediately of what bills you have sold."

The other Morris had actually achieved his objective and, indeed, while Salomon was unloading bills, Washington's soldiers were marching through Philadelphia on their way South. What had happened was this: Rochambeau had paid the Continental troops. Major William Popham noted that "this day will be famous in the annals of history for being the first in which the troops of the United States received one month's pay in specie."

The daily sixty-mile forced marches led to skirmishing from October 3 through 16 and then the ultimate convergence on Yorktown by Washington's and Rochambeau's ground forces and Comte de Grasse's fleet. Cornwallis surrendered on October 19, along with 8,000 other prisoners and 214 cannon. The English were left with Charlestown, Savannah and New York.

News of the battles and the victory did not travel quickly; good news never does. The Coffee-house in Philadelphia had been taken over by a group of Tories led by a physician, Abraham Chovet, who contended that Cornwallis could never be defeated. According to one commentator of unknown bias, this exchange occurred. "Being one day in the Coffee-house, just after the news of the capture of Lord Cornwallis at York Town had been received, he [Chovet] was accosted by a Jew Broker of the name of Solomon who in a rude manner went up to him and said with a sneer, 'Well, Doctor, I presume you know that your friend Lord Cornwallis is taken with all his army.' 'Do you believe it?' said Chovet. 'To be sure, I do,' replied the Jew. 'Well, my good friend, I can only tell you that you had better believe in Jesus Christ, that will save your poor soul from a worse fate than that of Lord Cornwallis, if, as you say, he has been captured.' The laughters were not on the side of the Israelite . . . The Jews were yet a hated and a despised race."[4]

*The Pennsylvania Packet*

October 27; November 10, 15;
December 6, 13, 18, 1781

*Haym Salomon, Broker,*
At his office in Front-street, between Market
and Arch-streets,
BUYS and sells Bills of Exchange on France, or any other part of Europe. Likewise all kinds of Merchandize. He also, discounts Bills or Drafts, and has it often in his power to procure Money on Loan for a short time.
Any gentlemen who may be pleased to favour him with their business, may depend on his utmost exertions for their interest; part of the money advanced if required.

# IV. The Jews of Philadelphia

Salomon had not heard from his parents for a long time and the news from Poland, brought by ship captains and then printed in the newspapers, was of upheavals and oppression. The Jewish quarter in Lissa had burned down in 1767. Five years later, there had been the first partition, with Prussia, Austria and Russia selecting plots of Polish ground to call their own. Then in January, 1775, the Jews had been expelled from Warsaw.

Worried, Salomon wrote to Gumple Samson at the start of 1782. Samson was an Amsterdam merchant and a relative of Jonas Phillips. Phillips had at one time sent him a copy of the Declaration of Independence (printed by Dunlap) and a letter written in Yiddish, and money for Phillips' mother. The packet had been intercepted by the British. The blockade was even tighter now that the land war was almost over, but Salomon wrote anyway, enclosing a bill of exchange for 500 guilders (about £1,500 Pennsylvania currency).

Salomon also committed himself to the Bank of North

America (the name decided upon for the National Bank), buying two shares for $800 specie. Sales had not gone well and barely two hundred of the thousand shares had been sold. Nonetheless, on January 5, 1782, an ad appeared in the *Packet*: "The Bank of North-America will open on Monday next." A shop had been leased from Tench Francis, Jr. It had a forty-foot front and was on the north side of Chestnut Street, west of Third. Morris and Washington attended the ceremonies; Thomas Willing was president of the bank and Tench Francis, cashier. Business hours were set at 10 to 1 and 3 to 5.

On January 8, Morris sent letters to the state governors. "The bank commenced its operations yesterday," he wrote. "It will facilitate the management of the finances of the United States. The several states may ... derive occasional advantages," such as in trade and payment of taxes. In *A Statement of the Accounts*, he added that the bank was necessary for "discounting notes of individuals, and thereby anticipating the receipt of public money: besides which, the persons who had contracted for furnishing rations to the army were also aided with discounts, upon the public credit." Morris had instituted a system of contracting, whereby a merchant would submit a bid to him for the supply of specific troops for a given period of time, usually a year.

A Partial List
of
First Subscribers to the Bank
subscription completed July 25, 1783
1000 shares at $400 specie each

| *Name* | *Shares* |
| --- | --- |
| Wm Bingham | 95 |
| John Holker | 5 |
| M. Hillegas | 1 |

| | |
|---|---|
| Luzerne | 1 |
| Robert Morris | 98 |
| Gouv. Morris | 1 |
| Isaac Moses | 1 |
| John Ross | 5 |
| John Swanwick | 71 |
| Haym Salomon | 2 |
| James Wilson | 5 |
| Thomas Willing | 11 |
| John Wilson | 2 |

After sending his letter to Gumple Samson, Salomon received one from Joshua Isaacs, a broker. About 2,000 of the British soldiers captured at Yorktown were in need of immediate cash. They were imprisoned in Lancaster, York, and Frederick Town, Pennsylvania. Isaacs did not have the money to give for the bills of exchange. On February 4, Salomon replied: "If the bills are drawn by the Paymaster general in favor of any particular officers and endorsed by the Commander-in-chief or at least by the Commanding officer of a Regiment for a short sight, payable in New York, they will answer. If they are drawn on London it will make no difference, if those answer that are drawn on New York. If they are drawn in the manner I have pointed out and I experience the Credit that they will have at New York, I shall be able to give you further information respecting them and if they entirely answer it will lay in my power to furnish cash sufficient to supply the whole army. If you will remit me some of them, and I find they will answer, I'll advance a small sum on them till I know their fate, which will be shortly after." Isaacs wrote back that the bills were acceptable. "I shall furnish you with as much cash as you may stand in need of," answered Salomon. "Proceed on the business immediately and draw on me for any Sum by post or express, it shall be honoured at Sight, let the Amount be ever so Great. The Bills may be drawn on New York or London if they are endorsed by their Commanding Officer."

Others needed cash. Don Francisco Rendon, the personal emissary of Carlos (Charles) III, King of Spain, had finally heard that the ship carrying his support money had been captured by the British. It was Salomon who gave him a loan, without the expectation of being repaid.[1] Closer to Salomon's desires was the issue of finally building a permanent synagogue for Mickveh Israel.

Before the war, there were almost 40,000 white people living in Philadelphia. Of that number, 100 were Jews. Services were held in a rented room in Sterling Alley, but there was no torah and no hazan. And the first group of Jews included those who either converted or intermarried.

Nathan Levy, son of the New York merchant Moses, arrived in 1735 and was soon working with Isaac Norris and then David and Moses Franks. His brother, Sampson Levy, became a Christian. David Franks married a Christian, although he remained involved with Jewish affairs. From the 1750s on, the interweaving of lives expanded dramatically. The Gratz brothers, Michael and Barnard, arrived from Upper Silesia. Barnard clerked for David Franks and married Richea, the daughter of the deceased Samuel Myers Cohen and his wife Rachel, née Levy. Cohen's daughter Rebecca was married to Mathias Bush, who would, in 1769, send men to collect forty pipes of wine from John Ross, the merchant-friend of Robert Morris, in payment of a debt. Another daughter, Elhalah, married the New York silversmith Myer Myers. And a son married the daughter of Joseph Simon, who lived in Lancaster, Pennsylvania.

In 1760, plans to build a synagogue fell through and so the next option was taken: Joseph Simon, Mathias Bush, Moses Mordecai, Barnard Gratz, Moses Heymann and Meyer Josephson wrote to Congregation Shearith Israel asking if they could borrow a torah. The request was granted. A few years later, there were the anti–Semitic attacks by Franklin's party during elections to the General Assembly, but even so Mathias Bush, Barnard and Michael Gratz, Benjamin Levy, Sampson Levy, Hayman Levy, Jr. and Moses Mordecai were signers of the nonimportation resolution of 1765, issued in protest of the Stamp Act. Seeking new trade outlets after that, Michael Gratz decided to ship meat to Jews in the West Indies. Abraham I. Abrahams sent down the certificate which proved the meat had been processed in a kosher manner. Then, in 1769, Gratz married Miriam, a daughter of Joseph Simon, thereby completing the family and business relations begun by his brother.

On July 25, 1771, the temporary synagogue was moved to the second floor of Joseph Cauffman's house on Cherry Alley, between Third and Fourth streets. The name Mickveh Israel was eventually settled on, with Barnard Gratz as parnas, Solomon Marache as gabay, and Michael Gratz, Henry Marks, Levy Marks, Moses Mordecai, Mordecai Levy, and Levi Solomon as the adjunta.

And so matters stood when the war began. During the occupation of Philadelphia, most of the Jews fled to Lancaster with the Continental Congress. David Franks remained, acting as a contractor for the British and opening his house to social events. His daughter Rebecca vied socially with Betty Shippen and, when the British were preparing to leave the city, was chosen a Queen of Beauty at the ball staged by Major André. On that occasion, she wore a low-cut polonaise dress, a spangled sash and, as was the fashion, a two-foot high wire frame on her head, to which were attached her hair, pearls and other jewels.

Then the British left, the vacuum being filled by General Benedict Arnold, his aid Major David Salisbury Franks, and the Continental army. David Franks was arrested and jailed briefly.

The exiled Jews returned. Down from New York came

57

Haym Salomon. Hayman Levy and Isaac Moses wrote to
hazan Gershom Mendes Seixas, who was still in Connecticut,
asking him if he would move to Philadelphia. He had recently
visited the city to perform the marriage of his brother, Benjamin, to Zipporah, a daughter of Hayman Levy.[2] Gershom
finally agreed, and the infrastructure of the synagogue was complete. The need for a building then became acute when
Cauffman told the Jews he no longer wanted them using his
house.

Jonas Phillips, who was at that time parnas, and Simon
Nathan, the gabay who had married Grace Seixas, the sister of
Gershom and Benjamin, called a meeting and opened subscriptions to raise the estimated £1,815 Pennsylvania currency
needed for construction of a synagogue. A paper was drawn up,
a "List of monies received by Mr Phillips for Offerings & Dona-
tions for Bilding of the Singogue. Subscribers names in
Philadelphia." Isaac Moses gave £22.10.0; Gershom Seixas,
£11.5.0; Benjamin Seixas, £38.5.6, and £43.11.6 for upkeep;
Salomon, £37.10.0. On the reverse side of the paper was this:

Note of the Gentlemen who Contributed
Largely First Subscription Donation

| | |
|---|---|
| Haym Solomons | £304.0.0 |
| Lopez & Riveras family | 62.12.6 |
| Isaac Moses | 112.16.6 |
| Hayman Levy | 80.0.0 |

The sum raised amounted to £897, or about £1,000 short
of the goal. Plans were made anyway to erect a temple on a
previously purchased plot situated next to a Reformed German
Congregation of "non–Israelites." In March, a meeting was held
at which members signed their names to a document stating
that "a Congregation to be known and distinguished by the

name of Mickve Israel" was then officially formed. Isaac Moses was elected parnas. The first order of business was to cope with the vehement objections of the German congregation to having a synagogue next door. Moses wrote them that "we wish to live in friendship with our neighbors" and offered them the land at purchase price.

So now the congregation had no land. An auction was arranged among the members, and bids were taken on the four cornerstones and two doorposts of the proposed temple. The highest bidders received prayers and honors. Enough money was raised for the purchase of a new lot on the north side of Cherry Alley or Street, near Third Street. Isaac Moses, Barnard Gratz, Hayman Levy, Jonas Phillips, Benjamin Seixas and Simon Nathan signed a bond for the builder. Members discussed a possible profiteering venture to cover the total cost of the temple: the tightened British blockade had pushed the cost of a barrel of flour from $5 in Philadelphia to $28 to $34 specie in Havana. Salomon joined in the venture.

The Jews weren't the only people rushing around trying to raise funds. If 1781 was a bad year, 1782 was going to be a terror. "On the first day of the year 1782," wrote Robert Morris in *A Statement of the Accounts*, "there remained in the treasury . . . about three hundred thousand dollars. A considerable sum was then due for past transactions . . ." In February, he placed advertisements in various newspapers reminding readers of the 1781 Congressional resolution recommending that the states "lay taxes for raising their quotas of money for the United States . . ." The money was to have been paid to a group of receivers selected by the superintendent of finance (Morris). The duties of the receivers were to urge payment of the taxes, accept Bank of North America notes in payment, purchase Bank of North America notes with monies received, publish monthly accounts in state newspapers, and give the receipts to the treasurer of the United States, Michael Hillegas.

Morris called in Salomon to see how the market was for bills. The next day, March 20, "Baron Steuben applied to me with Genl Washington's Letter for Pay &c and the absolute necessity of Supplying this Gentleman in order to enable him to do his duty appears so Strong that I am Compelled to advance Money for the use of this Department."[3] Five days later, Salomon informed Morris that "Bills of Exchange would be wanted this Week, my necessities will Compel me to draw and indeed I had already agreed last Week with Mr. La Caze and Mallet to Supply them with Bills for 100,000 Livres at 6/9d cash down for five Livres and as I shall want Money for the opening of the Campaign I have given Salomon leave to make Sale of 400,000 livres to be drawn at 180 days sight and the Purchasers to give notes payable at 60 days so that they may be discounted at the Bank price on the Conditions 7/ for five livres."

In the meantime, Morris went about arranging for a bank loan. In 1781, a combined French gift and loan totaling 10,000,000 livre ($2,000,000) was spent mainly in France to repay accumulated debts. The rest, $462,597 84/90, arrived in America on December 31 aboard the ship *Magicienne*. Morris used $151,981 28/90 of that money to purchase shares in the bank; the bank then authorized a loan of $300,000 (almost all of its capital), which was paid to Morris in short term bank notes at 6 percent interest.

Salomon had also been busy, selling forty-two bills of exchange with a face value of 500,000 livres for £34,758.18.2 Pennsylvania currency, which Morris hurriedly deposited with Hillegas at the Treasury.

*Letters of Robert Morris, April 8, 1782*

*To Haym Salomon*

You are to deliver unto Michael Hilligas Esq$^r$ Treasurer of the United States all the Notes which you have received from the Persons to whom you sold the Bills No. 1 to 42 amounting to L$^{vr}$ 500.000. sold for £34.758"18-2. Pennsylvania Currency agreable to the List of said Notes annexed hereto, you are to receive in Return Mr. Hilligas's duplicated Receipts specifying the Notes and Sums one of which receipts upon being produced to and deposited with Joseph Nourse Esq$^r$ Register of the Treasury will acquit you of this Claim, the other you may keep for your own Satisfaction and Security. You will render a separate Account of your Brokerage to Mr. Milligan the Comptroller and on his Certificate I will grant you a Warrant for the Amount.

*To Michael Hillegas*

You have herewith Enclosed my Order to Mr. Haym Salomon, to deliver you the sundry notes therein specifyed amounting to £34.758.18.2 Pennsylvania Currency being the Property of the United States received for Bills which I have drawn on Mr. Grand, Banker in Paris, you will give to Mr. Salomon such Receipts as mentioned in my Letter to him on which you will be charged in the Public Books for the amount, and as I shall have immediate occasion to Grant Warrants on you for the Current Expenditures of the United States you are hereby authorized to deposit these Notes with the Bank upon the customary Discount and the amount of the said Discount being duly certified must be admitted to your Credit and as a contingent charge on this Transaction.

*To Joseph Nourse*

You will receive herewith the Account Sales of forty two Setts of Exchange drawn by the Superintendent of

Promise to deliver the within certificate
regularly entered & made over to the Superintendent
in the ... House. Office withheld my hand
this 30 October 1782 —

Wayne ...

Finance upon Mons$^r$ Grand Banker in Paris No. 1 to 42.
amounting to five hundred thousand Livres Tournois
these Bills were put into the Hands of Haym Salomon
Broker who sold them with my Concurrence to Sundry
Persons in this City on thirty sixty and ninety days
Credit, he has the notes of the Persons to whom they
were sold amounting in the whole to thirty four thousand
seven hundred and fifty eight pounds eighteen Shillings
and two pence Pennsylvania Currency equal to 92,690
Dollars and 38/90ths. You will be pleased to charge
Haym Salomon for this Amount and Credit Mons.
Grand in a french account Current for the same — and
when Mr. Salomon shall produce to you a Receipt of
Michael Hillegas Esqr for the notes above mentioned
you will then charge Mr. Hillegas for the amount of those
notes crediting Mr. Salomon for the same. Salomon will
bring in an Account for his Brokerage separate for
Amount of which I shall gave him a warrant on the
Treasurer Mr. Hillegas will also have to discount the
Notes at the Bank but the Brokerage and discount may
be placed to Account of Contingent Expences whenever
the Amount is duly ascertained.

### Letter of April 26, 1782

Office of Finance

*Michael Hillegas Esqr.*

Sir,

You will receive enclosed herewith a Note of Hand
signed by Henry Hills Esq$^r$ promising to pay to my
Order six thousand seven hundred and fifty Pounds
Pennsylvania Currency equal to eighteen thousand
Dollars which I have endorsed payable to you or your
Order on account of the United States. Mr. Haym
Salomon Broker will deliver you Notes or pay you money
from Time to Time on account of Bills with which he is
supplied by me on Publick Account and this note of Mr.
Hills is in part Payment for such Bills so that you will

**Opposite: Sale of certificate by Haym Salomon.**

include the amount thereof in your Receipts to Mr. Salomon as he will be charged for the gross Amount of all the Bills sold and in Case the money be wanted for the discharge of my Warrants before the Notes fall due you are hereby authorized to discount the whole or any Part thereof.

I am Sir
Your most obedient and humble Servant
Robert Morris

The sea war took its annual turn for the worse, too. One of the stunts of the war had occurred on February 3, 1781, when Rodney's British fleet, strengthened by the loan of 5,000 men from Clinton's New York army, had captured St. Eustatius. By keeping the Dutch flags raised over the docks, the invaders were able to collect American ships until a more astute sailor noticed that those ships never left port after being unloaded. No stunt, however, was required of Rodney's fleet when, on April 12, 1782, it defeated de Grasse near the island of Sainte-Marie-Galante in the West Indies. De Grasse became a prisoner, and American trade in the area was demolished. The news reached Philadelphia in early May. Morris wrote General Benjamin Lincoln, the secretary at war: "[T]he operations of the campaign must stand still." The next day, May 8, he sent for Salomon, who "came and informs me that the interruption to our commerce and the losses of the merchants of this city has so disspirited the Purchasers of Bills of Exchange that he cannot make Sale at any Price." Morris wanted Congress to prod the states into complying with the year-old tax resolution, writing to the delegates: "I will make no new engagements, so that the public service must necessarily stand still . . . The fault is in the States. They have not complied with the requisitions of Congress."

That threat, of course, led to the resurrection of Arthur Lee's charges that Morris had profiteered at the expense of Congress while a member of the Secret Commerce Committee. James Madison and Benjamin Franklin came to the support of Morris and the matter was dropped.

One of Madison's friends and colleagues was Edmund Randolph. Randolph was leaving Congress, where he was a delegate, to return to Virginia to act as attorney-general. In March, Randolph had gone to Jacob Cohen for money and he, in turn, went to Salomon to broker a note dated March 17, drawn on Randolph in favor of Cohen. Randolph made it to Richmond and wrote Madison the rather sage observation of universal import that "I surely do not commit an unpardonable sin in reprehending my father for not handing down a fortune to me."

Not that Madison, who stayed on as a delegate from Virginia, was in any better position. Madison himself had approached the Jewish broker, who by now had taken on two clerks, James McCrea and Jacob Mordecai. On August 27, Madison wrote Randolph, "I cannot in any way make you more sensible of the importance of your kind attention to pecuniary remittances for me than by informing you that I have for some time past been a pensioner on the favor of H.S. Haym Solomon a Jew Broker."

Madison, however, continued to press Randolph for loans. In September, he noted in his diary, "I succeeded in getting the sum of £50 from Mr. Cohen, by depositing the obligation of Mr. Randolph, payable for at 60 days." It seems that Madison was averse to accepting money no-strings-attached from Salomon. As he wrote Randolph in late September:

> I am almost ashamed to reiterate my wants so incessantly to you, but they begin to be so urgent that it is impossible to suppress them. The kindness of our little friend in Front Street near the Coffee House is a fund which will preserve me from extremities, but I never resort to it

without great mortification, as he obstinately rejects all recompense. The price of money is so usurious that he thinks it ought to be extorted from none but those who aim at profitable speculations. To a necessitous Delegate he gratuitously spares a sǔpply out of his private stock.

Rachel gave birth to Sarah. The blockade and the loss of de Grasse threw a knife into the back of Mickveh Israel's dreams. The officers wrote to other congregations: "Our ability to complete the building is not equal to our wishes. Because of many recent losses we are under necessity to ask the assistance of our distant brethren."[4]

Morris also sought assistance. Steuben wanted money or he would quit being inspector of the army. Colonel Richard Butler wanted money for himself and his troops. On June 30, Morris had received another bank loan of $112,000; he used $12,000 as an installment against the prior loan and called in Salomon. "[T]he Broker informs me that he is applied to by Sundry Persons to sell Bills, I desired him to procure me Customers at 6/3d a Doll of 5 Livs . . . Haym Solomon proposed to me the Sale of Bills for Lrs.40,000 at 6/3d for Lrs 5 to be paid for as follows on the 11th July for Lrs 10,000, on the 16th July Lrs, 15,000 on the 1st August Lrs. 15,000." Salomon sold some bills "at 6/3d for five Livres, which I signed." By July 10, Morris had "authorized him to sell Bills payable in the First of August to answer Mr. Pierce's note."[5]

On July 12, Salomon asked Morris for permission to advertise his title. "This Broker," wrote Morris, "has been useful to the public Interest and requests leave to Publish himself as Broker to the office to which I have consented as I do not see any disadvantages can possibly arise to the public service but the Reverse and he expects individual Benefits therefrom."

A little over a week later, on July 20, the following

advertisement was printed in the *Packet* and *The Independent Gazetteer or, The Chronicle of Freedom:*

### HAYM SOLOMONS

Broker to the Office of Finance, to the Consul General of France, and to the Treasurer of the French Army, at his office in Front-street, between Market and Arch-streets, BUYS and SELLS on Commission

BANK Stock, Bills of Exchange on France, Spain, Holland, and other parts of Europe, the West Indies, and inland bills, at the useful commission. — He Buys and Sells

LOAN-Office Certificates, Continental and State Money, of this or any other state, Paymaster and Quartermaster General Notes; these and every other kind of paper transactions (bills of exchange excepted) he will charge his employers no more than ONE HALF PER CENT on his Commission,

He procures Money on Loan for a short time, and gets Notes and bills discounted.

Gentlemen and others, residing in this state, or any other of the united states, by sending their orders to this office, may depend on having their business transacted with as much fidelity and expedition, as if they were themselves present.

He receives Tobacco, Sugars, Tea, and every other sort of Goods to Sell on Commission, for which purpose he has provided proper Stores.

He flatters himself, his assiduity, punctuality, and extensive connections in his business, as a Broker, is well established in various parts of Europe, and in the united states in particular.

All persons who shall please to favour him with their business, may depend upon his utmost exertion for their interest, and — Part of the Money advanced, if required.

N.B. Paymaster-Generals' Notes taken as Cash for Bills of Exchange.

# V. The Revolution Winds Down

In 1780, Moses Cohen privateered with Samuel Judah and actually came up with a schooner full of Irish beef. On May 28, 1782, he proclaimed the establishment of an Intelligence Office. The *Packet*: "The Subscriber having observed the great and general utility of an Intelligence Office in populous and trading cities, begs leave to inform the Public, that he has opened an Office for that purpose, at his house on the east-side of Front-street, eight doors above Market-street; where persons wanting to purchase or sell Goods or Property of any kind . . . may enter and dispose of their respective articles at a moderate premium." Cohen also bought and sold bills and certificates and, for a fee of eighteen pence, he would act as an employment agent.

At about that time, soldiers started to return. Benjamin Nones, twenty-nine, born in France, had served as a private in Captain Verdier's regiment and then as a major on Washington's staff. He was soon discussing the possibility of a brokership with Myer M. Cohen. And Moses Benjamin Franks' son, Salomon's brother-in-law, drifted down from Massachusetts.

*The Gazetteer*

January 4, 1783

NONES and COHEN,
BROKERS.

At their Office in Front street, next Door to the Post-office, in the House formerly occupied by Mr. Philip Syng,
Transact every Kind of Business as Brokers, such as buying and selling Bills of Exchange on France, Spain, Holland, and other Parts; likewise Loan-Office and other Certificates, State Money of this and other of the United States: They will also receive and sell on Commission all Kinds of Dry and other Goods.

Their Employers may be assured of having their Business done on the most equitable Terms, Dispatch, and Punctuality of Payments.

Constant Attendance will be given at their office aforesaid, and at the Coffee-House, at the usual Hours of transacting Business there.

The Franks family was always involved in matters. David Franks had moved back to New York in 1780, occupying a house on Broadway in which British officers could again view his daughter, Rebecca. That same year found Isaac Franks as forage master for Westpoint Fort, which was ironic, because cousin David Salisbury Franks had been aide-de-camp to Benedict Arnold. Major André, who had given the Philadelphia ball at which Rebecca Franks had been honored, had been aide-de-camp to Sir Henry Clinton and coconspirator with Benedict Arnold. The plot had been to hand over Westpoint Fort, its ammunition, Washington, and Rochambeau. André, however, had been arrested by the militia, the plans found in his shoe, and the plot foiled. Arnold escaped by frantically rowing down the river towards the English frigate then anchored below Kingsferry. André was hanged. Major David S. Franks was arrested, tried, and acquitted, but since the suspicion of disgrace would never be completely erased from history, Franks moved for complete exoneration, which was granted in November.

In 1781, Isaac moved to Massachusetts and joined the Seventh Regiment. Rebecca succumbed to the advances of Lieutenant-Colonel Henry Johnston and, as announced in the *New York Gazette and Weekly Mercury* of January 28, 1782: "Last Thursday evening was married at her father's house in the Broadway, Miss Franks, youngest daughter of David Franks, Esq. to Henry Johnston Esq., nephew to General Walsh and Lieut. Colonel to the XVII Regiment foot."[1]

Isaac again moved, this time to Philadelphia. He was twenty-three and wished to be a broker. He took an office on Second Street between Market and Chestnut and began advertising in the *Packet* and *The Independent Gazetteer*. It was June of 1782. Half a year after Rebecca had married a Johnston, Isaac, on July 9, married Mary Davidson. Isaac also dropped out of Mickveh Israel.

*The Gazetteer*

January 11, 1783

Broker's Office, by
ISAAC FRANKS,

In Front-Street, two doors below the Coffee-House, Where all foreign and domestic negotiations, incident to the various branches of this office, are transacted upon truly moderate and liberal terms.

The utmost secrecy, candor, and fidelity to the interest of his employers, will be found (as usual) the leading principles in which he means to establish the confidence and approbation of a discerning public.

He buys and sells Bills of Exchange Upon France, Spain, Holland, or any part of Europe,

the continent of America, or West-Indies. Officers
Notes, Loan-Office Certificates,
    negotiated on the best terms. Money procured upon
such interest and
    security as shall be agreeable to the parties, either
for a month or a year. Promissory notes and bonds discounted or sold. Merchandise of every sort disposed of
upon the most advantageous terms, for which he has proper stores provided.
Houses and lands, bought, sold, or mortgaged. Continental and state money of this or any other
    state, bought or sold.
Whenever sudden emergencies require money to be
raised upon any paper security, merchandise, or produce, every effort will be used to accomplish it on the best
terms.
    By applying to the above, where the utmost atten-
tion will be paid to the interest of all those who may favor
him with their business, and nothing left undone that can
possibly be affected by fidelity, care, and dispatch.

Since a large number of paymaster general notes were to
fall due on August 1, Salomon was a frequent visitor to Robert
Morris during July. Salomon found some buyers among the
French. On the twenty-ninth, Salomon went to Morris "and
proposed a Sale of Bills to the Providore of the French Hospital
alleging that he has frequently sold him Bills on Credit and that
his engagements have always been punctually complied with
and after Consulting with Mr. G. Morris I agreed to supply him
with the Bills wanted." Those amounted to 120,000 livres.
Salomon brought them to the Providore, a Monsieur de Mars,
who summoned his friend, de Brassine. It was Brassine who
purchased some of the bills, giving Salomon a promissory note
for £3,514 Pennsylvania currency due November 1 and orally
guaranteed by de Mars.

*The Packet*

Saturday July 27, 1782

WARSAW,                                    February 28
THERE are more than 10,000 families of Jews established in this kingdom, to whom the kings have formerly
granted very considerable privileges, which, however,
through a course of time have been diminished, changed
or wholly revoked. This unhappy nation has been hereby
reduced to a very doleful condition. In this state of
distress, the Jews have at length ven tured to make a collection of all their privileges, and have repaired to this
capital in great numbers to reclaim them and procure the
king's confirmation of them. At present they can only
meddle with the sale of small wares or keep country ale-
houses, being wholly excluded from the culture of the
lands.

On August 16, Morris entrusted Salomon with the sale of
merchandise. "I sent for Haym Salomon and delivered him a
waggon receipt for twenty dry Hides sent by Geo. Albert Hall,
Esqur. from South Carolina and desired him to sell the same to
the best advantage of the United States. I also desired Salomon
to call on Colo. Miles for a few Casks of Pott Ash or Pearl Ashes
which I am informed are in his stores, being the property of the
United States and to sell the Same to best Advantage."[2] The rest
of the month was pretty moneyless. "August 28. Salomon the
Broker came and I urged him to leave no stone unturned to find
out Money—or the means by which I can obtain it."

On September 4, Salomon wrote to the firm Watson and
Cossoul in Nantes, asking them to trace the bill of exchange he
had sent Gumple Samson in January, money which had been
earmarked for his parents in Poland.

Mickveh Israel, on the other hand, was about ready for its
official opening. The temple was one story high of red brick;
thirty feet wide and thirty-six feet in depth. There were nineteen

73

windows. Two steps led to the Ark, and the platform, of pine, was seven feet by eight feet. Two hundred people could worship comfortably. Salomon contributed a scroll.[3]

The day before the consecration began a dispute which would continue for a number of months in the pages of the *Gazetteer*. Abraham Levy and his son Ezekiel, who had come to Philadelphia in 1768, were not doing well financially when Benjamin Nones, according to Abraham, began unfairly pressuring Abraham for commissions Nones claimed were overdue.[4]

On September 13, Salomon had the honor of leading the procession of Jews from Cauffman's home to the synagogue, where Salomon opened the door. It was a few minutes past three o'clock, the fifth of Tishri, 5543, the Friday before the Penitential Sabbath.

Salomon had forewarned Morris that John Chaloner and perhaps John Holker were again underselling bills, leading Morris to pay Chaloner[5] a douceur of 100,000 livre on condition that the broker promise to keep rates up. That was September 30, the same day Morris received another bank loan for $300,000 while repaying $300,000 on the previous loans. The total principal indebtedness remained at $400,000 specie. In Europe, John Adams was trying to persuade a group of Dutch firms to loan America 5,000,000 guilders ($2,000,000) at 5 percent interest. Franklin had raised 6,000,000 livre ($1,000,000) in Paris, but again most of the money would stay behind to cancel debts and when the remnant was shipped over, it would be on the ship carrying the preliminary peace documents.

General Carleton replaced Sir Henry Clinton as commander of the British forces and offered, in the name of the Crown, to acknowledge the independence of the United States if the states broke their alliance with France. That offer had been refused, initially to the satisfaction of the French. But then the French remembered the $2,000,000 per year in interest alone owed to them by the states, and Necker commented to Vergennes that perhaps America would be better off alone. Vergennes added to this thought in a letter sent to Luzerne in October. If the Americans, wrote Vergennes, "ask you for aid for the next year, say only that you are ignorant of the King's intentions . . . [W]e are astonished at the demands which they continue to make on us, while the Americans obstinately refuse to pay taxes." Luzerne then told Morris. Morris wrote Luzerne that "taxation requires time in all government and is to be perfected only by long experience in any country," thereby glossing over Morris' own frustrations without getting any money from the states.

It turned out that during this period Salomon himself was in financial straits, as were many of Philadelphia's Jews. It was Randolph who discovered that situation while seeking Salomon's advice concerning a debt owed by the state of Virginia. It seems that when Patrick Henry was governor of Virginia, he had a penchant for printing paper money (£1,500,000 worth), which helped lead to a 200 percent annual inflation rate later inherited by Thomas Jefferson, who became governor in 1779. A total of 1200 hands of tobacco had been borrowed from David Ross to keep Virginia's credit from sinking. Ross wanted to be repaid. Randolph approached Salomon to see if he had any ideas and instead came away shocked. He wrote to Madison on October 18: "I do not conceive there can be an objection to the application of the balance to the relief of the dependents of the little Levite." But there was no extra money. A month later, Randolph's letter to Madison was no more heartening. "I feel most sorely at this moment the wounds of Haym Salomon, and divers other jews of our connection in Philadelphia, and I clearly see, that my absence from home would throw me most terribly in the rear of the law." Randolph had similar worries: his father's creditors were unhappy.

The army, however, was the more bitter creditor. Towards the year's end, Morris found himself in the usual situation of scrambling to cover debts. He issued new notes to cover the government's immediate debit of $404,713; borrowed $200,000 from the bank; and paid back a $500,000 loan with $300,000 cash and $200,000 in bank shares owned by the government.[6] The army didn't care. Steuben, for example, was still pestering Morris for yearly stipends. Three days after Christmas, Steuben appeared at Morris' doorstep with Alexander Hamilton, who eloquently explained why Steuben should receive his desire. Morris suggested the two of them present their case to Congress. On January 2, 1783, the day began with a meeting with Salomon, during which the two discussed Salomon's account and the market for bills; then Steuben unexpectedly reappeared to announce that Congress had voted him a stipend of $2,400. Morris wrote out a warrant for that amount.

In the meantime, General Alexander McDougall and some other officers had sent a list of army grievances to Congress threatening "fatal consequences" if nothing was done.

Salomon had also become a creditor. Watson and Cossoul had replied that Gumple Samson had cashed the bill. Salomon wrote to Eleazer Levy, Hayman's son (who was then in Baltimore), asking if he knew someone in Amsterdam who could check up on Samson.[7] Levy wrote to Samuel Myers on January 9: "Some considerable time since, Mr. Salomon, reflecting on the Circumstances of his family in Poland, which when he left many years ago consisted of a Father, Mother, Brothers and Sisters, from whom he has not heard, thinking it his duty now as it is in his Power to afford them assistance he upward of a year ago remitted a bill on Amsterdam for Five hundred Guilders to Mr. Gumple Samson with directions where his relatives lived and how Mr. Samson was to dispose of the money among them. The main opportunities have offered and vessels arrived from Amsterdam Mr. Samson has not answered Mr. Salomon's Letter or in any manner acknowledged his receipt of the money remitted, the house on which the bill was drawn advise the bill was presented and the money paid by them to Mr. Samson ... Thus having related the Circumstances, you will judge of Mr. Salomon's anxiety to hear of his parents and his ardent wish to relieve them, for could he once know Mr. Samson was not inclined to trouble himself with this Charitable tho unprofitable commission Mr. Salomon would immediately use his utmost endeavors with some other people and remit another bill. — I need not enlarge further on this matter. Your own feelings will direct you what is necessary in order to accomplish relief to these poor relatives of Mr. Salomon, whose blessing must follow every individual that in any Shape is instrumental therein."

January of the new year had a few other twists left to it. The preliminary peace documents had been signed on November 30, 1782, and had reached the states in December. Trade and travel were loosening up. Late in December, Salomon had actually gone up to New York, still occupied by the British. He dropped in on the merchant William Vanderlockt and bumped into Lyon Hart. Lyon was the son of Jacob and Leah Hart. Leah was the daughter of the Philadelphia sexton Lyon Nathan. Jacob, a German and Talmudic scholar, had originally settled in Baltimore before moving to Philadelphia. On April 18, 1781, he had led the subscription drive for Lafayette's troops, which were about to depart on a campaign to harass Cornwallis. Jacob contributed £2,000 of the £5,000 raised and had the fortune of being repaid by Morris on May 27, 1782.

Salomon also met with Abraham Skinner, a lawyer who practiced before the Supreme Court of New York in Albany. On

77

January 1, 1783, Salomon loaned Skinner £800 New York currency right before departing for his return trip to Philadelphia.[8]

Over the next two weeks, Salomon and Morris had their usual meetings concerning the market for bills and the dire needs of the treasury. It seemed time for the Revolution to end or, at least, for the soldiers to go away, even if they were on one's own side. In any event, on January 24, 1783, Robert Morris did what any sane financier would have done years previously—he submitted his resignation as superintendent of finance to Congress.

# VI. An Army of Creditors

Morris, of course, had no choice but to stay on while Congress pondered his resignation. Salomon was involved in a French affair. First, he had just sold bills of exchange drawn on Monsieur Boutin, the treasurer of the Marine Department of France, and had guaranteed Boutin's credit with his own. Then it turned out that Gouvernor Morris, Robert Morris and himself had misjudged de Mars and his sidekick Brassine, who had absorbed the fever for profiteering but not the luck; they had thus spent the remainder of 1782 excusing nonpayment of the note and were now spending the beginning of 1783 in evasive measures. De Mars began acting as if he did not know Brassine. Salomon started researching de Mars' other transactions until stopped by Morris on February 22, who told Salomon "he may stop his enquiries until he hears farther from me as I am to have another Conference with Mr. De Mars on this business."

Salomon was selling houses, primarily on commission although he did own a vacant lot in the north ward.[1] He also

BON POUR, de 2900 Tournois    Pour Compte des Etats Unis de L'Amerique.

Philadelphie, le 24 Mars 1783.

Monfieur,

A trente    Jours de vue il vous plaira payer par cette fixieme de Change,
la premiere, feconde, troifieme, quatrieme, cinquieme, feptieme et huitieme ne l'etant,

a M _cui Denj-Parker_    ou a _fen_ Ordre

la Somme de _Deux Mille Neuf cens Livres Tournois_

Valeur reçue comptant que paſſerez fuivant l'avis de

Votre très humble ferviteur,

No. 121.

A Monfieur
Monf, GRAND,
    Banquier;
        A PARIS.

had "a couple of very likely Negro Boys" for sale on March 4. Lyon Hart wrote from New York that he wanted Salomon to ship him £1,800 New York currency worth of merchandise. Salomon put out feelers concerning the establishment of trade contacts in London.

Members of Mickveh Israel met and formed a Society for Destitute Strangers (Ezrath Orechim). Fifteen shillings to one pound Pennsylvania currency would be given any Jew arriving in Philadelphia who was in need. The loan could be repaid whenever the recipient had the money. Jacob Cohen was president of the Society, Isaiah Bush the secretary, and Salomon the treasurer.

When the congregation itself held elections, Simon Nathan became parnas, and the three trustees (the Ma'amad) were Asher Myers[2], Barnard Gratz, and Haym Salomon.

Then, on March 20, Morris told Salomon "that Mons[r] Tarle the Intendant of the French Army had peremptorily refused to pay the Note signed by Mons[r] De Brassine ... That Mons[r] De Mars the Chief of the Hospital Department had also refused Payment both of these Gentlemen alleging that Mons[r] de Brassine was not authorized to make such dealings or Engagements on Account of the Army ... Mr. De Mars being liable, I have directed Salomon to arrest him." Salomon first offered to make good the note himself since he had endorsed it, too, but Morris refused.

De Mars was arrested and, after one day in prison, confessed everything to Salomon. The trial date was set for April 26 in the Supreme Court. Morris hired his friend James Wilson to be the chief lawyer. Wilson, born in Scotland in 1742, had come to America in 1765 and nine years later, as the top lawyer

**Opposite: Bill of exchange signed by Robert Morris, March 24, 1783.**

81

in Pennsylvania, had joined the Committee of Correspondence of Cumberland County. Even though he signed the Declaration of Independence, he was considered a conservative and in October, 1779, his house at the corner of Walnut and Third was attacked by a frenzied militia, causing him to flee Philadelphia at the time.

Salomon's other French affair backfired without recourse. Boutin's credit was not good, and Salomon was forced to advertise in the *Gazetteer* and the *Packet* that he would fully back the Boutin bills endorsed and sold by him.

*The Gazetteer*

April 19, 1783

HAYM SALOMONS,

Takes this method to acquaint all those who possess full Sets of Bills of Exchange, drawn in his favour and indorsed by him, on Monsieur BOUTIN, Treasurer of the Marine Department of France, that they shall, on application, have the money refunded; and for Bills of the above description, which may have already been sent to France, satisfactory assurances will be given to the proprietors, that they shall be paid, agreeable to their respective tenors, in Paris.                    April 19.

Meanwhile, Eleazer Levy was visiting his father in Philadelphia prior to going to New York, where he planned to open a merchant's office. Salomon had finally received mail from Poland and dropped by to see if Eleazer could take instructions to Isaac Myers in New York concerning a response. Levy agreed. The letter dated April 29, reads: "I take the Liberty of sending you by Mr. Eleazer Sundry letters Rec'd from my Parents which I have to beg you to answer in the Best Manner you can and according to the Directions that Mr. Levy will give you. — I dare say you will partake with me of the Joy that I feel in receiving these letters so long wished for and in relieving their necessity. By you will [I] answer the four letters & also please to write duplicates of each, which in so doing you will confer an obligation . . . Please to mention to my father the difficulties that I have labored under in not having any learning, and that I should not have known what to have done had it not been for the languages that I learned in my travels, such as French, English, etc. Therefore I would advise him and all my relatives to have their children well educated, particularly in the Christian languages and should any of my brothers' children have a good head to learn Hebrew [I] would contribute toward their being insructed."

David Tevele Horachow, rabbi in Lissa since 1774, was preaching against assimilation, the German *haskalah*.

The trial of de Mars took place on a Saturday, and Morris was triumphant from the witness stand, castigating de Mars without mercy. The verdict was guilty. By May 1, Salomon was able to tell Morris "that he had received the Money for Mons$^r$ de Brassine's note of Mons$^r$ de Mars and that he will discharge the same at the Bank. He says he paid the Tavern Charges of the Court and Jury the Cost of Subpoenas and serving then on Witnesses I desired him also to pay the Lawyer's Fees and bring one Account for the whole."

Salomon interrupted that affair to visit New York. The synagogue, Shearith Israel, was open. The temporary parnas was Alexander Zuntz, who was commissary and agent to the general staff of the Hessians and husband to Abraham I. Abrahams' daughter, Rachel. Salomon's business, though, was to pick up a promissory note for £1,000 New York currency from Lyon Hart.

Back in Philadelphia, Salomon deposited the de Mars money and received a draft in its stead. He then visited Joseph

Greenway, who had become captain of a regiment attached to the First Battalion, Philadelphia County Militia, commanded by Col. John Shee. Salomon joined the regiment.[3] Salomon then went over to Wilson, who demanded five half Joes for his legal opinion in the trial and ten half Joes for having served as prosecutor. A Joe, or Portuguese Johannes, was a gold coin worth slightly more than a pound sterling. Morris wanted to negotiate further, since if Wilson received fifteen half Joes, all the lawyers who had been even tangentially involved would each demand the same. Wilson, however, made Morris back down on May 21 and Morris told Salomon to pay the man. The total cost of the trial came to $414 14/90.[4]

Salomon may have become somewhat more suspicious of his fellow debtor due to the above experiences. At the beginning of June, he dispatched the following to William Vanderlockt: "Your favor of the 1st instant I have rec'd inclosing a draft on Jno. Holker esquire for 200 dollars which has been accepted. Am Exceedingly Sorry to hear of your Illness but have since heard to my inexpressible joy that you are likely to recover which may be the case is the Sincere wish of your obedient & very humble servant. N.B. You may remember that you In-dorsed Some time ago a note of Charles Erdmans for 225 Dollars which note was given me and put in the Bank but was not Honoured by Mr. Erdman when due But would not make any disturbance on acc't of your name being on it. I therefore beg you will let me know what to do & if you have no objection will sue him tho he has promised to pay it when he Gets money the only look upon that as an excuse to retard the payment of it."

The army was apparently thinking the same thoughts about the Congress. Gathered in Lancaster, the soldiers chanted their grievances and suddenly burst forth in an amoebalike surge towards Philadelphia. At that moment,

84

Salomon was writing business letters, bent over his desk on the second floor of the building which also housed his office. One to Joseph Haines of Virginia: "I hope you'll excuse my writing so short a letter as a Multiplicity of Business hardly gives me time to think what I am doing, though nothing shall ever induce me to forget my friends. Please to allow Capt. Craven the 14 dollars. I would not give him the trouble of Swearing to it. His word is Sufficient."

There was a noise in the distance, which did not go unnoticed within the Congressional halls. Salomon jotted another letter.

Philadelphia, 20 June, 1783

Mr. Bart M. Spitzer
   Charlestown,
     South Carolina

Sir:
     I am surprised after the many assurances that you gave me of writing to me that you have not done it. However, will admit this as an Excuse that your whole time is devoted to the Ladys and can't spare time to inform a friend of your welfare, however desirous he may be of hearing. — I doubt if the Ladys here have the same reason to complain of your neglect. Am certain you would not make it long before your return were you to know how desirous the Ladys are of your presence and one in particular who wishes that no pecuniary views may get the better of the partiality you always entertained for her. Time will not permit me to enlarge but be assured that you may command anything that is in the power of your
Obe't Servant

The delegates probably wished they were with the "Ladys," since the enraged soldiers had surrounded the hall and were cat-calling at the leaders. Salomon wrote a letter of warning to a friend. "Last week arrived a Mr. Pollack from Cape Francis who lodges at Mr. Jacobs & If I have any penetration he would willingly become your Rival and asure you he would be no despicable one if Money can recommend him but as to anything else he is a second Mose Nathan." Moses D. Nathans was a wealthy Jewish merchant-broker who lived, unmarried, with a nonjewess and had had children with her.[5] There were ladies, and then there were ladies, and there were the men.

Elias Boudinot of New Jersey was president of Congress. He had a house on Chestnut Street, between Fourth and Fifth. He was not thinking of that warm home, though; he was shouting out proposals on adjourning the Congress right then to a state or city or anywhere as far away as feasible. The delegates had trouble hearing him due to the furor outside.

To a cousin, Philip Moses, Salomon wrote: "I expected ere now you would have honoured me with a line if it was only to assure me of your safe arrival and welfare which I have heard with pleasure from other people but could have been much more pleasing to have been assured of it from yourself. Inclosed have sent you the copys of Sundry letters from my parents & am afraid I would wrong your friendship was I not convinced that you'll share with me the Joy I feel in hearing from my parents after so long an absence, A Joy more easily conceived than expressed & in relieving them in their indigent Circumstances which by God's blessing I hope to enable them to live above want for the future. By the inclosed you'll Perceive that we are Related to one another which acc't is so Satisfactory that there is no reason to doubt the authenticity of it And any Commission that you may have this way will execute them with double pleasure, as my being related enhances the friendship I always Entertained for you & in expectation of a Speedy Answer I subscribe myself Your friend & humble Servant."

86

It was evening. Boudinot had succeeded in getting the delegates to agree to adjourning Congress to reconvene June 26 in Princeton, which seemed a sufficient distance. The delegates exited the hall with trepidation. For some reason — certainly not awe — the soldiers parted and the delegates passed through the hungry, unpaid sea.[6]

A few days later, Salomon received word from Boudinot: Sell the house on Chestnut Street. Salomon tossed that commission in along with the beeswax, deerskins and ginseng he also had on the market at that time, although he never considered himself a merchant. As he wrote to John Strettell, a London merchant: "I am to acquaint you that I do not profess Mercantile abilities and therefore the punctuality and Precision Requisite in that Line cannot be complied with on my part ... I mentioned my commencing a small establishment with your house to Mr. Cad. Morris. It appeared satisfactory to him, and he will mention me to you in the Course of his Correspondence. My business is a broker and chiefly in bills of Exchange and so very extensive that I am generally known to the Mercantile part of North America."

His name was also becoming well known in Poland in association with money. An uncle, Joseph Elis, wrote requesting a yearly allowance and information on the odds of a Talmudic scholar making a fortune in America. Salomon replied negatively to each on July 10. "Rich I am not, but the little I have I think it my duty to share with my poor father and mother, for they are the First to be provided for by me and must and shall have the Preference. Whatever little more I can squeeze out I will give my relatives but I tell you plainly and truly that it is not in my power to give you or any relative yearly Allowances. Don't you or any of them expect it — don't fill your mind with vain expectations and golden Dreams that can never be accomplished. I have three young children and as my wife

**Sale of certificates by Haym Salomon.**

is very young may have more, and if you and the rest of my
relatives will consider things with reason they will be sensible of
this I now write. But notwithstanding this, I mean to assist my
relatives as far as lies in my Power." After telling him that the
Talmud would not help him financially in the states, Salomon
enclosed six guineas in the letter and sent another fifty guineas
via Gumple Samson in Amsterdam, with whom Salomon had
patched up the prior misunderstanding that had probably been
caused by the typical delays and poor communications of the
times.

Salomon also was approached to lend his name to a petition
written by Thomas Paine and directed to the absent Congress.[7]

Salomon did sign it. It read, in part, "We beg leave to assure Congress that if either now or at any future time until the Residence of Congress shall be permanently established it should appear to your Hon^rble Body that the situation of Philadelphia is convenient for transacting therein the concerns of the Nation that Congress may Repose the utmost confidence in its inhabitants. . . ."

*The Gazetteer*

July 26, 1783

> Wanted, a Couple of Clerks, Who are well acquainted with business, and understand book keeping, and that can be well recommended, as none else need apply; if they understand French, will be more acceptable. Inquire of HAYM SALOMONS, Broker.
> Philadelphia, 8th July, 1783.

June had ended with Morris receiving another bank loan of $83,194 while returning the remaining government shares in the bank, valued at $53,394 — shares which were eventually resold in Holland. But the notes Morris was issuing to the army were going to start falling due. Morris called for Salomon on September 15 and "desired he would immediately enquire and inform me what Price can be had for Bills on Amsterdam at 90 Days Sight." The next day: "Salomon says he cannot get more than 3/ per Guilder for Bills. I told him to sell some at that price." Salomon was able to sell G 40,000 at 3/ per, 90 days' sight.

At the end of September, Morris repaid $29,800 to the bank and received another loan of $54,781, leaving an outstanding balance of $154,781. Morris had issued notes worth $1,401,000 in April and July and was about to write out another $602,000 for October. But the bank was through with lending money to the government. Even though the bank had been chartered by Congress on March 26, 1782, it was considered a state creature. The charter granted it by Pennsylvania, after all, had some legality and a sense of longevity behind it; the charter issued by Congress was a piece of paper of unknown value, if any. The government, having returned the last of its bank shares, had nothing more in the way of collateral except the potentiality of receiving tax money from the states. But that had been a potential for almost two years. The bank could no longer invest its funds in unsound loans. So it was that by the end of October, Morris told Salomon "that he should dispose of no Bills but for the Money, that the Bank would no longer discount for this Office and therefore the Public Bills must be sold for Cash only, and more especially as there were but few remaining to be disposed of." When word came that John Adams had obtained an Amsterdam loan, even though at high interest rates,[8] Morris hurried to Princeton to confer with Vanderkele, the minister plenipotentiary of the United Netherlands, and Congress, eking out a promise that the money would go towards the debts troubling Morris. Before leaving, Morris was told by Washington that the final peace treaty had been signed on September 3 but, instead of waiting for Congressional ratification, Washington fully intended to order the army disbanded on November 3.

*The Packet*

November 20, 1783

Haym Salomon, Authorized Broker to the Office of Finance, &c. has now to dispose of at his OFFICE in Front-street (where he transacts, in the most extensive manner, every branch of business relative to his profession)

BANK STOCK

The various sorts of Certificates, Notes, &c. issued by the public; Bills of Exchange upon France, Spain, Holland, England, Denmark, Hamburgh, &c. and the principal West-India islands; and can drawn bills upon most of the principal places on this continent.

He receives every species of Merchandize to sell upon Commission; for which purpose he has provided proper stores; and procures freight for vessels. Any person residing in this or any of the United States, who will send their orders to his office, may depend on having their business transacted with as much fidelity as if they were themselves present.

He flatters himself his assiduity, punctuality and extensive connections in his business, as a Broker, are well established in several parts of Europe, and the United States in particular.

All those who shall please to favour him with their business, may depend upon his utmost exertions for their interest, and part of the money advanced, if desired.

He has also for SALE

The Square bounded by Chesnut, Walnut, Seventh and Eighth streets; a Lot upon the east side of Seventh street, between Market and Arch streets; the Slate House (as it is called) and Lot, at the corner of Norris' alley, in Second-street; nearly opposite to the City-tavern; three Houses in Norris's alley, adjoining the State-House lot; two contiguous Lots at Kensington, one of them being part of Batchelor's-Hall lot; the House on the north side of Chesnut-street, between Fourth and Fifth-streets, lately occupied by his excellency, the president; the elegant House and Lot in the same street, in which the French ambassador lives; one in Arch-street; two in Second-street, one of them near the corner of Chestnut-street, in a good stand for business; one in Market-street, an excellent stand; a genteel retired one in Walnut-street; and a small Lot in the same street, nearly opposite to the Post-office, which would be a good situation for a store or office; an excellent well built stable (which might be easily turned into a store) and Lot in Union street; a Tract of Land situate in Berwick township, York county, lying on Little Canewage creek,

and containing 200 acres; and several other tracts and
Plantations in Pennsylvania and the Jersey.

A house in Market-street and a lot in the same
street; a three story house and lot in Chesnut-street, and
two three story houses on the west side of Moravian-
alley.

The terms of payment will be made extremely
easy.                                      Nov. 19th

While the British were preparing to evacuate New York,
Salomon was preparing his own invasion. He purchased a
house and lot at No. 22 Wall Street, owned by Francis Lucas
and rented by Anthony L. Bleecker & Sons. It was time to close
up shop in Philadelphia, particularly by unloading merchandise
and real estate. For example, he had the "Slate House . . . at the
corner of Norris' alley" in which William Penn had lived. The
French ambassador's house in Chestnut Street was Luzerne's.
And there was the home "lately occupied by his excellency" and
current resident of Princeton, Boudinot.

# VII. Jews, Politics and Business

Lazarus Barnett and Lyon Moses came from Amsterdam and set up shop "Five doors above Arch-street, in Second-street." Moses was a "Dutch Broker," Barnett the assistant, and the two sold goods and bills on Holland during the summer of 1783. Samuel Hays moved in with the Salomons as clerk and apprentice to Haym, whose other clerk was Jacob Mordecai. Jacob was the son of Moses Mordecai, who had settled in Philadelphia in 1750 and become a merchant and broker. Jacob had previously clerked for David Franks during the British occupation. When Salomon was considering his eventual move back to New York, he turned to Jacob and asked whether he would be his partner. Jacob was twenty-one, Salomon forty-three. Moses Cohen, who had privateered with Samuel Judah in 1780 with a certain schooner full of Irish beef, now sold houses at Pennington, eight miles north of Trenton. He joined with Benjamin Nones to form Benjamin Nones and Comp. Brokers, still in Front Street at the house formerly owned by Philip Syng and then by Nones himself. Jonas Phillips, located near the Coffee-house on the south side of Market Street, sold merchandise on commission and had several vacant lots available near the Hospital. Barnett achieved bankruptcy and fled Philadelphia. Lyon Moses succeeded him, going into business in Race Street, between Third and Fourth, opposite the King of Prussia Tavern. On the twenty-fifth of November, the British left New York and the Jews began leaving Philadelphia.

Before leaving, though, other matters came to a head. A freeman of Pennsylvania could not sit in the General Assembly after his election unless he vowed to "acknowledge the Scriptures of the old and new Testament to be given by divine inspiration." A Jew, therefore, could run for office, win, and be unemployed nonetheless.[1] The officers of Mickveh Israel, which included Salomon, sent a petition out on December 23: "To the honourable the COUNCIL of CENSORS, assembled agreeable to the Constitution of the State of Pennsylvania. The Memorial of Rabbi Ger. Seixas of the Synagogue of the Jews at Philadelphia, Simon Nathan their Parnass or President, Asher Myers, Bernard Gratz and Haym Salomon, the Ma'amad, or Associates of their council in behalf of themselves and their brethren Jews, residing in Pennsylvania."

The petitioners pointed out the contradiction between the oath of office and the second paragraph of the state's bill of rights, which read "that no man who acknowledges the being of a God can be justly deprived or abridged of any civil rights as a citizen on account of his religious sentiments." Jews, they wrote, "are as fond of liberty as their religious societies can be," and there was nothing in Jewish law which would disturb the "safety and happiness" of the state. Jews owned property, paid taxes, and during the Revolution contributed as much as any other religious society in terms of soldiers, losses and allegiance, "in proportion to the number of their members." Even though they might not wish to serve in government office, "yet the disability of Jews to take seat among the representatives of the people, as worded by the said religious test, might determine their free choice to go to New York, or to any other of the United States of America, where there is no such like restraint." The reference to New York was because Article XXXVII of the 1777 State constitution read ". . . the free exercise and enjoyment of religious profession and worship, without discrimination or preference, shall for ever hereafter be allowed within this State to all mankind." The oath of office did not mention the Bible: "I _____ do solemnly swear and declare, in the presence of Almighty God, that I will bear true faith and allegiance to the State of New York, as a good subject of the said State, and will do my duty as much as such a subject ought to do."[2]

The day the petition was sent, Jonas Phillips' "Chair-house in Laetitia-court alley" was broken into and, although nothing was stolen, his chaise, sulkey and harness were damaged.[3] Three months later, worse was to happen, but for the time being, the Council of Censors tabled the petition.

On December 31, Morris closed the government's account with the bank by repaying $154,781. The bank was planning to expand by opening another subscription of 1,000 shares at $500 a share. But there were rumors that a group of merchants wished to start a competing bank. Their leader was Edward Shippen, a moderately wealthy man who owned eight and a half acres of land in Passyunk Township, one horse, one cow, two slaves, and who was joint owner of the City Tavern on Second Street along with Henry Hill and John Wilcox. One of Shippen's supporters was Thomas Fisher, a Quaker, who worked with his brothers Samuel and Miers — Miers was a renowned Tory during the Revolution — and their father, Joshua, in the firm Joshua Fisher and Sons, selling European goods. Another

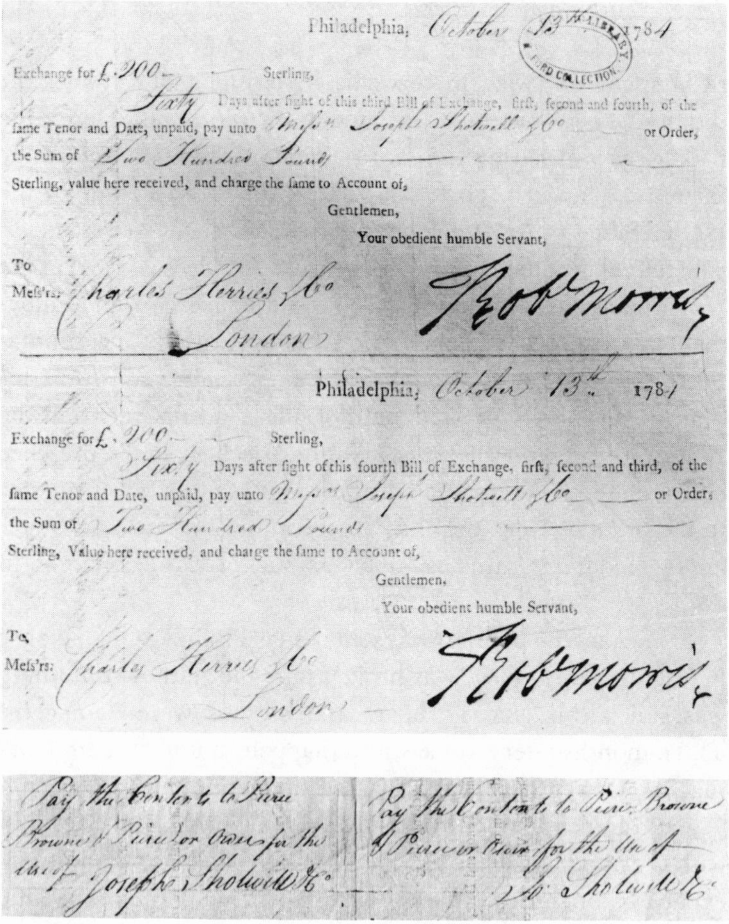
Philadelphia, October 13th 1784

Exchange for £ 200 Sterling,

Sixty Days after sight of this third Bill of Exchange, first, second and fourth, of the same Tenor and Date, unpaid, pay unto Messrs Joseph Shotwell & Co or Order, the Sum of Two Hundred Pounds Sterling, value here received, and charge the same to Account of,

Gentlemen,

Your obedient humble Servant,

Robt Morris

To Mess'rs Charles Herries & Co London

Philadelphia, October 13th 1784

Exchange for £ 200 Sterling,

Sixty Days after sight of this fourth Bill of Exchange, first, second and third, of the same Tenor and Date, unpaid, pay unto Messrs Joseph Shotwell & Co or Order, the Sum of Two Hundred Pounds Sterling, Value here received, and charge the same to Account of,

Gentlemen,

Your obedient humble Servant,

Robt Morris

To, Mess'rs Charles Herries & Co London

Pay the Contents to Pierce Browne & Pierce or Order for the use of Joseph Shotwell & Co

Pay the Contents to Pierce Browne & Pierce or Order for the use of Jo. Shotwell & Co

**Morris note, front (top) and back, October 13, 1784.**

supporter was Tench Coxe, a merchant with a store on Front Street, near Union Street.

On January 12, 1784, when the bank issued the new shares, Salomon bought two for himself and ten for De Heyder, Veydt & Co., a firm on Second Street between Race and Arch which sold European goods. A week later, the proposed bank announced it would sell 700 shares at $400 each.[4] The Bank of North America closed its subscription, assessed the situation, and then went back into the market with a price of $400 for its shares.[5] Salomon was commissioned by William Bradford to purchase four of the new bank shares for Joshua Maddax Wallace.

On February 10, Salomon reported to Morris that "Edward Shippen and others chosen President and Directors of a new Bank lately instituted in Opposition to the national Bank have presented a Petition for a Charter of Incorporation." The case was to be argued by Miers Fisher before the State Assembly in early March.

On February 16, Salomon, along with his family and a package of dispatches from Morris to various people, traveled to New York. Salomon and Jacob Mordecai reached final agreement on the partnership. The house at 22 Wall Street would be the office. On February 21, Salomon mortgaged the premises to William Rhinelander. Salomon and Rachel co-signed two notes, one for £3,000 New York currency, the other a draft on Daniel Parker & Co. for £1,200 due May 1 with interest of £37.6.8.

Salomon returned to Philadelphia in time for Miers Fisher's presentation on the proposed Bank of Pennsylvania. The reason the bank was needed, Fisher told the Assembly, was that the Bank of North America was swayed by the influence of Jews, who favored outrageous interest rates and who oppressed people in their hideous drive for wealth. This infiltration of Jewish evilness would be halted if another bank were established based on just interest rates.

Salomon replied on March 13 in the *Gazetteer*.[6] "Your conspicuous *toryism* and *disaffection* long since buried you in the silent grave of *popular* oblivion and contempt." The statements were "indecent, unjust, inhumane aspersions . . . I am a Jew, it is my own nation and profession. I also subscribe myself a Broker . . . I exult and glory in reflecting that we have the honour to reside in a *free* country . . . and I do not at all despair, notwithstanding former obstacles, that we shall still obtain other privilege that we aspire to enjoy along with our fellow-citizens. It also affords me unspeakable satisfaction . . . to contemplate that we have in general been early uniform, decisive whigs, and were second to none in our patriotism and attachment to our country!" Jews were not the "authors of high and unusual interest." Indeed, "those very persons who are now flattering themselves with the idea of a new Bank first invented the practice of discounting notes at five per cent." The article was signed A JEW BROKER.

On March 16, the directors of the Bank of Pennsylvania withdrew their charter application from the Assembly.

*The Gazetteer*

April 10, 1784

Haym Salomon, Broker,
Wants as an Apprentice, a lad of about sixteen years of age. He must be of a good family, write a tolerable hand, and be well recommended, none else need apply.
Undeniable Bills of Exchange
Upon Baltimore, Richmond and Charlestown,
To be had at Haym Salomon's Office.
Philadelphia, April 2, 1784.

When Salomon returned to New York on another journey, he carried the usual dispatches for Morris and a letter of

reference from Gouvernor Morris addressed to Chancellor
Robert R. Livingston.[7] Gouvernor highly recommended
Salomon "because upon a long Acquaintance with him in his
business I have the best reason to know his Capacity and to
believe in his Fidelity. Permit me to add, that he has always
been a decided Wig [sic]." Salomon obtained an auctioneer's
license and an extension on the payments due William
Rhinelander. He neglected one errand, which he corrected on
his return to Philadelphia by writing the officers of Shearith
Israel and asking if they would send small lamp branches to
Mickveh Israel.

*Gazetteer* and *Packet*

May 15, 18, 1784

### HAYM SALOMON,
*Broker to the Office of Finance,*
Having procured a license for exercising the employment
of Auctioneer, has now opened, for the reception of every
species of merchandise his house, No. 22, Wall-Street,
lately occupied by Mr. Anthony L. Bleecker (one of the
best stands in the city) and every branch of business,
which in the smallest degree appertains to the professions
of FACTOR AUCTIONIER and BROKER, will be
transacted in it with that fidelity, dispatch and punctuality, which had hitherto characterised his dealings

The house, in point of convenience and situation, is
exceedingly well calculated for the different kinds of
business above mentioned: and he thinks it almost un-
necessary to assure those who may favour it with their
orders, that the strictest attention will be paid to them,
and the utmost care and solicitude employed, to promote
their interests.

The nature of his business enables him to make
remittances, to any part of the world with particular
facility, and this he hopes will operate considerably in his
favour, with those who live at a distance and desire of

ment.

## HAYM SALOMON,

*Broker to the Office of Finance,*

HAVING procured a licenſe for exerciſing the employment of Auctioneer, has now opened, for the reception of every ſpecies of merchandiſe, his houſe, No. 22, Wall-ſtreet, lately occupied by Mr. Anthony L. Bleecker, (one of the beſt ſtands in this city) and every branch of buſineſs, which in the ſmalleſt degree appertains to the profeſſions of FACTOR AUCTIONIER and BROKER, will be tranſacted in it with that fidelity, diſpatch and punctuality, which has hitherto characteriſed his dealings

The houſe, in point of convenience and ſituation, is exceedingly well calculated for the different kinds of buſineſs above mentioned: and he thinks it almoſt unneceſſary to aſſure thoſe who may favour it with their orders, that the ſtrickeſt attention will be paid to them, and the utmoſt care and ſolicitude employed, to promote their intereſt.

The nature of his buſineſs enables him to make remittances, to any part of the world with peculiar facility, and this he hopes will operate conſiderably in his favour, with thoſe who live at a diſtance.

A deſire of being more extenſively uſeful and of giving univerſal ſatisfaction to the public, are are among his prinnipal motives for opening this houſe, and ſhall be the great leading principle of all its tranſactions.

By being Broker to the Office of Finance, and honored with its confidence, all thoſe ſums have paſſed through his hands which the generoſity of the French Monarch, and the affection of the Merchants of the United Provinces, prompted them to furniſh us with to enable us to ſupport the expence of the war, and which have ſo much contributed to its ſucceſs and happy termination. This is a circumſtance which has eſtabliſhed his credit and reputation, and procured him the confidence of the public, a confidence which ſhall be his ſtudy and ambition to merit and increaſe, by ſacredly performing all his engagements.

The buſineſs will be conducted upon the moſt liberal and extenſive plan, under the firm of HAYM SALOMON, and JACOB MORDE-CAI

"The New York Journal and State Gazette," Thursday, December 16, 1784.

being more extensively useful and of giving universal satisfaction to the public, are are among his principal motives for opening this house, and shall be the great leading principle of all its transactions.

By being Broker to the Office of Finance, and honored with its confidence, all those sums have passed through his hands with the generosity of the French Monarch, and the affection of the Merchants of the United Provinces, prompted them to furnish us with to enable us to support the expence of the war, and which have so much contributed to its success and happy termination. This is a circumstance which has established his credit and reputation, and procured him the confidence of the public, a confidence which shall be his study and ambition to merit and increase, by sacredly performing all his engagements.

The business will be conducted upon the most liberal and extensive plan, under the firm of HAYM SALOMON, and JACOB MORDECAI.

*N.B.* Part Cash will be advance, if required.

Salomon was entering the twilight of life, and the events surrounding the Revolution — the types of events of which few ever get to hear and in which fewer still get to participate — were over.

# VIII. Jews and Freemasonry

Those manipulators of stone who wandered from country to country with their complex tools, hewing Gothic buildings engraved with intricate symbols, were masons. They measured themselves by degrees based on an architecture of esoteric philosophy. In 1716, there were four lodges in or near London. These united to form the Constitutional Grand Lodge, which adopted constitutions written by Dr. James Anderson. The preface declared that Moses was a Grand Master. The early Jews were masons. Further, "a Mason is oblig'd, by his Tenure, to obey the Moral Law; and if he rightly understands the Art, he will never be a stupid Atheist, nor an irreligious Libertine . . . to be *good Men and true*, or Men of Honour and Honesty, by whatever Denominations or Persuasions they may be distinguish'd."

By 1738, the Grand Lodge was in decline. Pope Clement XII had issued a bull, *In Eminenti*, which had threatened excommunication for any Catholic who became a mason. The Great Schism occurred in 1751, when Lawrence Dermott, an Irishman

103

living in England, formed the Ancient or Atholl Grand Lodge. Dermott wanted to restore "old customs and rituals" and confer the Royal Arch degree. The schism became known as Ancients *vs.* Moderns. Dermott gave his Grand Lodge an edge by freely handing out the warrants which permitted groups to call themselves lodges.

The masons hit America in 1682, in New Jersey. By the time of the Revolution, there were seven lodges, five Modern ones in Massachusetts, Pennsylvania, North Carolina, South Carolina and New York, and two Ancient ones, in Massachusetts and Pennsylvania.

Webb, a Master of the Grand Lodge in Rhode Island during the late eighteenth century, gives some insight into masonry in his description of the two middle degrees. While Solomon was King, Webb explains, some workmen murdered Hiram, King of Tyre, and fled Jerusalem. Solomon selected by lot nine "brethren" who sought the group's leader. One of the nine eventually found and killed the man. Solomon rewarded the whole group by naming them Elected Knights, which is the eighteenth degree. Similarly, fifteen other men chased the remaining criminals and became Elected Grand Masters, the nineteenth degree. The oath of an Elected Knight was, "I do solemnly swear, in the presence of Almighty God, that I will revenge the assassination of our worthy master, Hiram Abiff, not only on the murderers, but also, on all who may betray the secrets of this degree." Each degree had its own oath of secrecy and each had its own symbolic penalty, growing ever worse. The penalty was pantomimed — for example, pretending to slit the throat — by the member to introduce himself as a freemason. Degrees also carried their own trappings: jewelry, such as a compass with gold plate, a five point star, compass and square, level, plumb rule, book, scroll, arms and chest, or dove and olive branch; and aprons. An Entered Apprentice wore white lambskin. A Fellow Craft wore white lambskin with two sky-blue rosettes at the bottom. A Master Mason could have three rosettes, a sky-blue lining and fringe, and silver tassels.

Parades and processions were common, such as the one held in Philadelphia on Monday, December 28, 1778, to celebrate the anniversary of St. John the Evangelist. George Washington and three hundred other masons attended, marching to Christ Church.

Lodges tended to attract like-minded people. Saint Andrew's Lodge, in which Paul Revere was an up-and-coming member, allowed revolutionaries to use its meeting hall, the Green Dragon.[1] The Grand Lodge of New York had Tory leanings and dissolved when its Grand Master, Sir John Johnson, became a British army officer in 1776. But there was one essential quality to the masonic society which was uncommon in America and most of the world: Jews could belong and attain positions of leadership. Further, to become a member of Washington's staff, it was said that one had to be a mason.

Popular Masonic Song
*Early 19th Century*

Hail masonry DIVINE!
Glory of ages, shine,
　　Long may'st thou reign,
Where'er thy lodges stand,
May they have great command,
And always grace the land,
　　THOU ART DIVINE!

Glorious Art! which fires the mind,
With sweet harmony and love,
Surely thou wast first designed.
A FORETASTE OF THE JOYS ABOVE!

Still louder Fame! they trumpet blow,
Let all the distant regions know,

Freemasonry is this; —
*Almighty wisdom gave it birth*
And Heaven has fix'd it here on earth,
A TYPE OF FUTURE BLISS!!

Moses Michael Hays was born in 1739 to the New York merchant Judah. The two later worked together, keeping a receipt book, and expanding their contacts to Newport. Moses' sister, Reyna, eventually married that congregation's rabbi, Isaac de Abraham Touro. Moses was parnas of Shearith Israel in 1768. When he finally moved to Newport, during the summer of 1776, he was accused of being a Tory by the Rhode Island Assembly. But he had already taken the loyalty oath to the Revolution. When called to testify, he asserted his belief in America even though, since he was a Jew, he was not allowed to vote. Afterward, he sent a letter requesting vindication and exoneration.

Hays was a mason. He opened the Newport Lodge to which a dozen Jews belonged, including Isaac DaCosta. Down in New York, Jonas Phillips was a master mason in Trinity Lodge #4 F. & A.M. (Free and Accepted Masons) by 1760. Others raised at about that time were Simon Nathan, Myer M. Cohen, Samuel Myers, and Benjamin Seixas. Jacob Hart was raised in Baltimore Lodge #16 F. & A.M. in 1776. Benjamin Nones was a mason by 1779.

*A Partial List of Jewish Masons*

| Name | Position Attained | By |
|------|-------------------|-----|
| Solomon Bush | Deputy Inspector General for Pennsylvania | 1781 |
| Moses Cohen | Knight of the Sun | 1781 |
| Moses Cohen | Master Mason | 1784 |
| Myer M. Cohen | Knight of the Sun | 1781 |
| Isaac DaCosta | Grand Warden Inspector General for West-Indies | 1781 |
| Jacob Hart | Master Mason | 1776 |

| Name | Position Attained | By |
|------|-------------------|-----|
| Moses M. Hays | Deputy Grand Inspector General; Grand Master of the Grand Lodge of Massachusetts | 1780s |
| Ezekial Levy | Master Mason | 1781 |
| Samuel Myers | Deputy Grand Inspector for Leward Islands | 1781 |
| Simon Nathan | Deputy Grand Inspector for North Carolina | 1781 |
| Benjamin Nones | Master Mason | 1779 |
| Jonas Phillips | Master Mason | 1760 |
| Benjamin Seixas | Prince of Jerusalem | 1781 |
| Haym Salomon | Master Mason | 1784 |

An interesting case was Solomon Bush. A member of the Pennsylvania Militia, he was shot in either the arm or the leg and taken prisoner during the battle of Goshen Township, September 18, 1777. Two years later, he was promoted to lieutenant colonel. In 1780, however, he sent a memorial to Congress requesting the position of secretary to the Board of Treasury, since the war wound made active duty painful. The memorial, like Haym Salomon's, went unanswered. Bush was appointed Deputy Inspector-General for Pennsylvania masonry and, in 1785, became Grand Master. It was in that role that he corresponded with another Grand Master, Frederick the Great of Prussia, who did not particularly like Jews.

The minutes of Philadelphia Lodge No. 2, F. & A.M.[2] state that on June 21, 1784, "An E.A. [Entered Apprentice] Lodge opened, and by virtue of two Dispensations from the R.W.G.M. [Right Worshipful Grand Master] in favor of Ashton Humphres and Haym Solomon, were balloted for, approved and Entered." The oath Salomon took for the first degree was this: "I, A.B., of my own free will and accord, in presence of Almighty God, and this worshipful Lodge of Free and accepted Masons, dedicated to God, and held forth to the holy order of St. John, do hereby, and hereon, most solemnly and sincerely promise and swear, that I will always hail, ever conceal and never reveal, any part or parts, art or arts, point or points of the secrets, arts and mysteries of ancient Freemasonry, which I have received, am about to receive, or may hereafter be instructed in, to any person or persons in the known world, except it be to a true and lawful brother mason, or within the body of a just and lawfully constituted lodge of such; and not unto him, nor unto them whom I shall hear so to be, but unto him and them only whom I shall find so to be, after strict and due examination or lawful information. Furthermore do I promise and swear, that I will not write, print, stamp, stain, hew, cut, carve, indent, paint or engrave it on any thing moveable or immoveable, under the whole canopy of Heaven . . . Binding myself under no less penalty than to have my throat cut across, my tongue torn out by the roots, and my body buried in the rough sands."

The initiation rite would have included a symbolic confrontation with death, such as being stabbed with a fake knife or "hung."

Salomon became a master mason after the usual waiting period of two months.[3]

*Minutes of Lodge No. 2, F. & A.M.*

June 23, 5784. Transactions. — An E.A. Lodge opened. By Virtue of a Dispensation from the R.W.G. Master, Capt Joseph Walker, was balloted for, and approved. When he and Haym Solomon were Entered. Lodge closed.

A.F.C. Fellow Craft Lodge opened in form, when Bros. Humphreys, — Walker and Solomon were passed to the degree of F.C.

Lodge closed in harmony at 10 o'clock —

August 9, 1784. An A.E. Entered Apprentice Lodge

opened — Lodge closed. — A Masters Lodge opened, when Bro. Hyman Solomon, was raised to Sublime Degree of Master Mason. —

### A Partial List of Masons[4]

| Name | Lodge | State | Date |
|------|-------|-------|------|
| Benedict Arnold | Hiram Lodge No. 1 | CT | 1765 |
| Benjamin Franklin | — — | PA | 1730s |
| Thomas Jefferson* | Virtue Lodge No. 44 | VA | — |
| Lafayette | — — | — | 1770s |
| James Madison | — — | — | 1795 |
| Robert Morris* | — — | — | 1760s |
| Casimir Pulaski* | Military Lodge | GA | — |
| Edmund Randolph | Williamsburg Lodge No. 6 | VA | 1774 |
| Paul Revere | St. Andrew's Lodge | MA | 1760 |
| Arthur St. Clair | Nova Caesarea Lodge No. 10 | OH | — |
| George Washington | — — | VA | 1750s |

Salomon was also a believer in air travel. During the 1770s, there were two flying machine companies in the New York–New Jersey–Philadelphia region, charging from three to twenty shillings per trip by air balloon. In the summer of 1784, Dr. John Morgan published appeals for subscribers for capital to build a balloon sixty feet high, fifty feet in diameter, and using 1,200 yards of India-Persian silk. Ascension was scheduled for July 4. Haym Salomon was a contributor. The balloon did not take off as planned; a Mr. Carnes of Maryland rushed his to completion but, unfortunately, that launch was not a success. Morgan nonetheless reopened subscriptions July 31, much to the

---

*Not known for sure. Morris, for example, was given a masonic apron by Washington in 1778. Washington, of course, was sworn to the presidency on a masonic Bible, and his funeral was in the masonic tradition.

accolades of Benjamin Franklin, who was a distant admirer in Paris.[5]

Salomon, meanwhile, became embroiled in a legal dispute. Ephraim Abraham died intestate and his business partner, Jacob Cohen, had himself appointed executor. Abraham had been an Indian trader, a member of Philadelphia's Northern District City Guards during the Revolution, and a Virginia merchant. His next of kin and heir, Jacob Abraham, lived in Lissa. Cohen decided that the heir was too far away to bother with and did not send him any of the estate. Abraham enlisted the aid of Rabbi David Tevele Horachow, who wrote to Salomon. Cohen would not listen to Salomon, until Salomon was given power of attorney for the heir. Salomon dictated a letter to Joseph Carpeles, who had recently arrived from Prague, for dispatch to Tevele. "2nd of Elul, 5544. Oh friend who is enlightened in all his ways, whose knowledge equals his keenness; famous abroad for his learning; teacher, master and Rabbi; celebrated for his genius and wisdom, whose name is praised among the Jewish people everywhere—Rabbi David Tevele, may his light shine on forever. Your letter of the first of last Kislev, as well as the power of attorney and the testimony of the heir Reb Jacob, were duly received. I did not let the matter rest but hurried to communicate these things to Reb Jacob Cohen, Esquire. Upon seeing your letter he changed his mind and said to me as follows: 'You need not go to court over this matter. I shall permit examination of my books that pertain to the period of partnership with the deceased Reb Ephraim. From this you will be able to draw up a current account and I shall pay you what I owe the heir Reb Jacob.' Almost every day I took leave of my business (which is quite extensive) in order to fulfill your command and speedily finish the matter."[6] Cohen had agreed to arbitrate. Carpeles represented Salomon. Simon Nathan, the parnas of Mickveh Israel, represented Cohen. Each side put up

4,000 ducats (approximately £2,000 Pennsylvania currency) as a bond. Cohen was ordered to pay 800 ducats in judgment.

In that same letter, Salomon wrote, "I also attended to the matter of my father's clothes, the membership in the community and the burial plot. I have written to Gumple WB, Esquire, to send my father fifty ducats for this purpose, as my father mentions in his letter ... May I also trouble you to speak to my mother, may she live long, concerning the gold chain which I gave her. I wish it to be understood that this is a gift given on condition that it must be returned, so that she shall not be able to sell it. I desire also that vigilance be constantly exercised in this connection so that the heir as well shall be prevented from selling it."

Salomon returned to New York to attend to business — he had not yet made the final break with Philadelphia, partly because of business and partly because Rachel was again pregnant. New York had passed a law whereby religious societies could incorporate. In May, Myer Myers, Hayman Levy, Solomon Simson, Isaac Moses, Solomon M. Cohen and Benjamin Seixas had been elected trustees. They incorporated Shearith Israel in June. The real problem was again rowdiness in the temple, and on Thursday, the 23rd of Elul, "Jacob Mordecai and Hyman Solomons" attended a meeting at which Levy proposed changing the congregation's constitution to promote decorum and harmony.[7]

Salomon also told Mordecai to order £3,000 (New York currency) worth of merchandise for the store. Isaac Moses approached Salomon and asked him to serve as his agent in Philadelphia. Moses had 27,000 acres of land in Tryon County, New York, divided into lots that could be purchased with New York certificates (bonds). Eleazer Oswald, publisher of the *Gazetteer*, was already serving as an agent.

*The Gazetteer*

August 28, 1784

New-York Securities.

A GENTLEMAN, a native of Philadelphia, and has a handsome property in that city, who is well acquainted with the lands in the state of New-York, and particularly those at Skeensborough, Mohawk river, Otiego, and Oneida lakes, will discover and undertake to place those securities on some of the best lands in that state, at 15 per cent. premium for his trouble, clear of all expences, to be paid either in lands purchased, or public securities. It is apprehended these proposals will be deemed reasonable as well as advantageous, to the holders of such securities in Pennsylvania, who are not acquainted with the lands now offered for sale in the state of New-York. A line directed to A.B. and left with the certificates at Mr. Eleazer Oswald's, or Mr. Haym Salomon's, broker, at Philadelphia, will be duly attended to.

August 23, 1784

At the end of November, Salomon was again in the city. Mordecai had received and paid for the merchandise and sought reimbursement from Salomon, who drew a note for £3,000 in Mordecai's favor and dated it December 1. Then Mordecai told him that some members of Shearith Israel were thinking of forming a Society for Dispensing Acts of Kindness (Hebra Gemiluth Hasadim). The two men had their names placed on the list of contributors.[8]

# IX. Salomon's Death

Salomon was forty-five years old. He had three children when he became terminally ill and, as the sickness lingered, he watched Rachel give birth to a son, named after him. He died on Thursday, January 6, 1785. He was buried in the cemetery of Mickveh Israel, and on Yom Kippur eve, the congregation recited a Sephardic *hashcabah* (memorial prayer) in his honor.

*The Gazetteer*

January 8, 1785

Thursday last, expired, after a lingering illness, Mr. HAYM SALOMONS, an eminent broker of this city; he was a native of Poland, and of the Hebrew nation. He was remarkable for his skill and integrity in his profession, and for his generous and humane deportment. His remains were yesterday deposited in the burial ground of the Synagogue, in this city.

Salomon might have been amused at the fact that he was "deposited" for safe-keeping in the Mickveh Israel cemetery and

113

might have been further amused at an ensuing Congressional enactment of August 6, 1956, 70 Stat. 1074, providing that "the Mikveh Israel Cemetery, located in Philadelphia, Pennsylvania, and containing the graves of Haym Salomon and other outstanding patriots of the Revolutionary War who played important parts in the early history of the United States, shall be declared to be a unit of the Independence National Historical Park: Provided, That the United States shall not thereby assume any responsibility to provide for the administration, care, or maintenance of said Mikveh Israel Cemetery." He would not have been amused at the fact that he died intestate soon after seeing what that situation could lead to, even between partners.

# Epilogue: An Intestate Fiasco

"On Thursday, died Haym Salomon, a broker," *Pennsylvania Journal*, January 8, 1785
"Robert Morris, a golden calf worshipped by the aristocratic Junto." *Jack Retort*

After the letter testamentary had been filed in Philadelphia, the appointed administrators — Eleazer Levy was one — placed announcements in the local papers, and an inventory was taken. The same process had to be repeated in New York because Salomon owned property there, too. Levy became an administrator in that proceeding. Mordecai, the young partner, did not act with any grace towards the bereaved family. As soon as he. had heard of Salomon's death, he had declared a "private sale" of those goods for which Salomon had recently given his note.

*The New-York Journal and State Gazette*

January 20, 1785

J. MORDECAI,
No. 22, *Wall-Street,*

115

*Has to dispose of at private sale,*
White and brown Havanna Sugars,
    Muscovado ditto,
Gin in cases and hampers,
Brandy,
Sherry,
Fyal and               Wines, in tierces, pipes and
Malaga                      quarter-casks,
Hyson,
Green,
Souchong,
Congo &              *Teas.*
Bohea
Toys assorted in boxes,
Tiles, ditto,
Pepper,
A large assortment of seasonable Dry Goods.

---

UNDOUBTED BILLS OF EXCHANGE on England and Holland, FOR SALE. — Apply as above.

*The Packet* and *The Gazetteer*

Mid-January to February, 1785

ALL Persons indebted to the estate of Haym Salomon, late of this city, Broker, deceased, are requested to make payment; and those who have demands against the said estate, are desired to deliver them properly attested, to
        Rachel Salomon, Administratix
        Thomas Fitzsimmons
        Matthew Clarkson
        Eleazer Levy        Administrators
        Joseph Carson
Philadelphia, January 14, 1785

*The Packet*

Mid-February to March, 1785

    The administrators to the estate of HAYM SALOMON, desirous of paying the demands against said estate, and closing their administration as soon as possible, give this public Notice to all persons indebted to the said estate, that if they do not pay the sums by them respectively due, or give satisfactory assurance to the administators withins one month from the date hereof, that their obligation — and accounts will then be put into the hands of an attorney, to be proceeded upon according to law.

Phildelphia, February 11, 1785

*The New-York Journal and the General Advertiser*

February 24, 1785

ALL persons having demands against the late copartnership of H. SALOMON and J. MORDECAI, are desired to produce their accounts, that they may be adjusted and paid: — And those indebted are requested to make immediate payment to

JACOB MORDECAI,
surviving partner of H. Salomon
and J. Mordecai

When Rachel and Eleazer Levy began to sort out the estate, Mordecai presented the note and demanded payment of £3,000 for "divers goods wares and merchandizes." Levy and the other administrators in New York claimed that they paid the note, but Mordecai later filed suit in the New York Supreme Court.

There were other suits. The administrators hired Aaron Burr, one of the busiest and best known of the New York attorneys, to both defend and prosecute in the Chancery Court, the Court for the Correction of Errors, and the Supreme Court.[1] The inventory which was eventually filed listed a minuscule £210 New York currency as Salomon's assets for that state. The inventory for Pennsylvania showed a debit of $500.[2] Yet when Rachel returned to Philadelphia, a letter dated

117

September 7 from Benjamin Nones and Moses Cohen awaited her. It sought £15 Pennsylvania currency, to be paid to "Mr. Manuel Josephson Presidt. of the Jewish Synagogue of this City," money which was claimed to be "the Property of the Society called Hezrat Orechim."[3]

In October, Samuel Hays, Salomon's former clerk and apprentice, opened an office on Front Street, announcing that "By a long residence with the late Mr. Haym Salomon, he has acquired a perfect knowledge of this business."

To return to the lawsuits, Mordecai was represented by Brockholst Livingston in the state Supreme Court held in Albany during the July, 1786 session. The defendants were William Constable, Alexander Robertson and James A. Stewart, "Administrators of the Goods and Chattels rights and Credits which were of Haym Salomon late of the City of New York Auctioneer deceased." Mordecai's claims were for £3,000 N.Y. currency pursuant to a note which Salomon had issued in Mordecai's favor; £6,000 for goods; £6,000 on a prior loan; and £3,000 in general arrearages. When issue was finally joined in July, 1787, Burr rejected the claims outright on a number of grounds. First, the estate had been fully administered before Mordecai brought suit. Second, Mordecai's rights of tenancy at No. 22 Wall Street were questionable since the mortgage had been in Salomon's name. Last, Burr ingeniously argued that Salomon had satisfied the alleged debts on January 6, 1785. No mention was made of the fact that Salomon had died that day in Philadelphia.

Mordecai, however, was not yet cowed. A writ of venire was issued to the sheriff, commanding him to gather "twelve free and law full men"—that is, men with a freehold, messuages, tenements or an estate valued at £60—to hear the case. The initial writ was for a hearing calendared in Albany for October, 1787. The sheriff did not find the twelve men. New writs were issued for trials scheduled in New York City for January, April, July and October of 1788, and January, 1789, with similar results. But at the April, 1789 session, Mordecai did not appear, thereby defaulting. The administrators were awarded £21.1.9 for costs and charges.

Burr took the offensive against Lyon Hart and Abraham Skinner. In October, 1785, "Alexander Robertson, William Constable, James Stewart and Eleazer Levy administrators of . . . Haym Salomon Deceased at the time of his Death who died Intestate put in their Place Aaron Burr their attorney against Lyon Hart in a Plea of Trespass on the Case . . . Whereas the said Lyon Hart on the Second day of May in the year of our lord one thousand seven hundred and eighty three at the City of New York in the North ward of the said City was indebted to the said Haym Salomon in his life time in one thousand Pounds of lawful money of the State of New York for diverse goods wares and Merchandizes by the said Haym Salomon in his life time before that time Sold and delivered to the said Lyon Hart . . ." Another £800 was owed "for the work labour care and diligence" of Salomon.

Hart, too, was represented by Brockholst Livingston, but by January, 1786, Livingston appeared on the side of the plaintiff-administrators, since Hart had not paid legal fees which were due and owing. Poor Hart was represented by George Bond in the plea of debt. This sheriff, Robert Boyd, was successful in delivering a jury on the writ of venire. Hearings were held before Chief Justice Richard Morris. By March 16, Hart acknowledged himself bound to pay his debts and promised to pay what he could on or before March 17. On March 18, Bond filed an admission of nonpayment. The beleaguered merchant was arrested and "delivered to Bail on the taking of his Body — — ."

Skinner was luckier in that he delayed his payment for

twenty years. But then, Skinner was a lawyer. In July, 1785, the administrators, through Burr, filed a plea of trespass in Albany, claiming £800 in moneys owed and £1,000 in damages. Skinner failed to appear at the January, 1786 session. The sheriff, Marinus Willet, was commanded to find a jury. Willet was unable to do so, but by that time, Skinner was prepared to admit his guilt. The administrators entered judgment. Skinner entered a writ of error in the Court for the Correction of Errors, which was composed of the president of the state senate, senators, and Chancellor Robert R. Livingston. On February 19, 1787, that court declared that Skinner's tactic was for delay only and ordered further sums to be added on to the prior judgment to serve as damages for that delay. Skinner paid up, but when he did so, it was 1805.

The more poignant case involved No. 22 Wall Street. Salomon and Rachel had cosigned the notes. They were not fully paid by Salomon's death. For some reason, the mortgagee, William Rhinelander, did not bring suit for quite some time. On February 1, 1788, Rhinelander had Mordecai evicted from the house, which was then rented out to Anthony Bleecker, who had occupied it before Salomon had purchased it. A.L. Bleecker & Sons sold hops, Madeira, tea, lots and dry goods, and paid Rhinelander a quarterly rent of £40.

It was not until 1791 that Rhinelander decided to foreclose and, when he brought suit, he petitioned the Court of Chancery to have guardians appointed for Salomon's children, whom Rhinelander believed were living in Philadelphia. Ezekiel was 13, Deborah 11, Sarah 9, and Haym M. 6. On July 23, Rhinelander amended his request since some of the children were living in New York. Which of the children and the cause for the split up are unknown. In any event, Chancellor Robert R. Livingston granted the appointment of commissioners, who were to assign the guardians. The suit itself was against Rachel,

120

her new husband, David Heilbron, and the children. Sheriff Marinus Willet was given a writ commanding the seizure of the house and its sale. Advertisements were run by the sheriff in *The Daily Advertiser* beginning on October 15 and ending six months thereafter.

On December 1, the house was sold for £2,510 to John Broome, a former alderman and a partner in Broome, Platt & Co. of No. 190 Water Street; John Delafield, broker and auctioneer at No. 5 Queen Street; William Laight, at that time campaigning for alderman in the third ward; and Guilian Ver Planck and John Watts, both merchants. Rhinelander then submitted an accounting to the court, claiming a deficiency due and owing of £1,872.1.2. He was paid, and the defendants were released from debt.

And that was the life and aftermath of Haym Salomon and of the Revolution. On August 24, 1786, Rachel married the previously mentioned David Heilbron, whose name was also spelled Halbrun or Halburn, and who was apparently a Scottish Jew. Little is known of their marriage except that they lived in New York for a while.

As for the children, Ezekiel Salomon became a merchant and then branch manager of the United States Bank in New Orleans, where he died suddenly. Sarah married Joseph Andrews, who had been born in Strassburg in 1753 and who was a teacher and member of Shearith Israel when they met. They later moved to Philadelphia. There is no record of what happened to Deborah.

Haym M. Salomon, the last born, became a merchant. In 1811, Rachel conveyed power of attorney to him. In 1821, Haym went to court and was awarded the complete administration over his father's estate. He began a crusade of recognition for his father. Searching for documents, he wrote to Joseph Nourse, who had been register of the Treasury during the

Revolution. Nourse wrote back that "I have cast back to those periods when your honored father was agent of the Office of Finance, but the inroads of the British army in 1814 deprived us of every record in relation to the vouchers of the period to which I refer."

James Madison wrote, "Among other members of Congs. from Virginia whose resources public & private had been cut off, I had occasion once perhaps twice myself to resort to his pecuniary aid on a small scale for current wants. We regarded him as upright intelligent and friendly in his transactions with us."

Haym presented what letters and documents he could find to Congress and petitioned for repayment of money which he claimed the government owed his father.[4] He gradually changed his demands to land, then less money. Haym died towards the end of the Civil War.

There is a statue of Salomon in Chicago. It was designed by Lorado Taft and Leonard Grunelle and was paid for by the Patriotic Foundation of Chicago. Completed December 15, 1941, it shows Salomon, Robert Morris and George Washington. The three look extremely grave. On March 25, 1975, a ten-cent postage stamp was issued in Salomon's honor. He is depicted as a man wearing a white wig which could not distract attention from the large nose. He is wearing a red jacket and holds a quill in his right hand. Behind him are three silver and one gold coins. The caption is: "Contributors to the Cause . . . Haym Salomon, Financial Hero." The back of the stamp reads: "Financial Hero. Businessman and broker Haym Salomon was responsible for raising most of the money needed to finance the American Revolution and later to save the new nation from collapse."

As for the others, Moses M. Hays moved to Boston, bought a house on Hanover Street, gave to the poor and loved children. He died wealthy. Moses Cohen moved from Second and Chestnut to the east side of Second Street, next door to James Gallagher, in Philadelphia. Jacob Hart gave away his daughter, Hendla, in marriage to Haym M. Salomon. Jonas Phillips returned to New York.[5] Between 1816 and 1822, Gershom Seixas, Benjamin Seixas, Isaac Moses, Alexander Zuntz, Jacob Hart, Simon Nathan, Eleazer Levy and Rachel Heilbron all died, everyone except Rachel being buried in the Shearith Israel cemetery.

Washington, Adams and Madison became presidents. James Wilson became a United States Supreme Court justice, an alcoholic, and a debtor. He died in prison. Then there was Robert Morris.

Morris was finally able to leave office in November of 1784. He speculated in land. The result was bankruptcy and imprisonment. When John Wallace of Philadelphia sent a copy of the *Account of Robert Morris' Property* to George Bancroft of New York, he enclosed a letter, dated May 25, 1803. "You will understand that it is his Return of property after he was put in gaol here and desired to be relieved under the bankrupt law. It shews the large scale of his operations—their wholly disastrous issue; and the reasons, in these, and in the ruin which they brought to many persons in our city." The collapse of Morris' firm—Morris, Greenleaf and Nicholson—seriously affected Alexander Hamilton, John Jay, Bishop White, Thomas Willing, Albert Gallatin, and George Harrison. Morris' account was a list of betrayals by John Holker ("This Gentleman took it into his head . . . that he could recover large Sums of Money of me"); John Paterson ("This villain deceived and cheated me"); and William Bingham. The government claimed a balance due from the contracts made between Willing, Morris & Co. and the Secret Commerce Committee. The Bank of North America, his creation, claimed that he was overdrawn.

And then there were all the personal Morris notes which could not be paid.

Morris was rescued from the Walnut Street prison by Gouvernor Morris, who tended to him in Morrisiana, New York, until Robert was well enough to return to Philadelphia. For the next five years, Gouvernor sent Robert an annuity. Then that need, too, ended.

# Appendix: Documents from the Settling of Salomon's Estate

*Letter of Testament, Haym Salomon,*
*Filed with the New York Court of Probates July 20, 1785*

The People of the State of New-York, by the Grace of God, Free and Independent.

To Rachel Solomon of the City of Philadelphia Widow & Eleazer Levi, James Stewart William Constable, and Alexander Robertson all of the City of New York Merchants Friendly or Creditors of Hyam Solomon late of the City of Philadelphia merchant deceased — send Greeting:

Whereas The said Hyam Solomon as is alleged, lately died intestate, having whilst living, and at the Time of his Death, Goods, Chattels, or Credits within this State, by Means whereof the ordering and granting Administration of all and singular the said Goods, Chattels and Credits; and also the auditing, allowing and final discharging the Account thereof, doth appertain unto us; and we being desirous that the Goods, Chattels and Credits of the said Deceased, may be well and faithfully administered, applied and disposed of, do grant unto you the said Rachel Solomon, Eleazer Levi, James Stewart, William Constable and Alexander Robertson full Power by

these Presents, to administer and faithfully dispose of all and
singular the said Goods, Chattels and Credits, to ask, demand,
recover and receive, the Debts which unto the said Deceased,
whilst living, and at the Time of his Death, did belong; and to
pay the Debts which the said Deceased did owe, so far as such
Goods, Chattels and Credits will thereto extend, and the Law
require, you being first duly sworn, well and faithfully to administer the same, and to make the exhibit a true and perfect
Inventory of all and singular the said Goods, Chattels and
Credits; and also to render a just and true Account thereof,
when thereunto required: And we do by these Presents ordain,
depute and constitute you the said Rachel Solomon, Eleazer
Levi, James Stewart, William Constable & Alexander Robert-
son Administrators of all and singular Goods, Chattels and
Credits which were of the said Haym Solomon — — — — — — —
IN TESTIMONY whereof, we have caused the Seal of our
Court of Probates to be hereunto affixed:
WITNESS Thomas Tredwell Esquire, Judge of our said
Court, at the City of New York the Twentieth Day of July in
the Year of Our Lord, One Thousand Seven hundred and
Eighty five.

Dav. Judson C$^{lk}$

## Conveyance from Rachel to Haym M. Salomon

In 1811, Rachel gave Haym M. power of attorney for the estate.
Ten years later, Haym claimed administration of it. In the Letter of
Administration, the names of the original administrators are given
followed by the phrase "now also deceased." That does not make clear
whether all of them are dead, or just Alexander Robertson. Rachel
would have been in her mid-sixties; the other merchants, probably
older than her.

\*\*\*

## Conveyance

Recorded for and at the Request of Mr. Haym M.
Salomon this 18$^{th}$ day of June 1811 at ½ past 10 o clock P.M.
KNOW ALL MEN BY THESE PRESENTS that I Rachel
Heilbron widow late Rachel Solomon administratrix of Haym

Salomon DO make Constitute and appoint my son Haym
M Salomon of the City of New York Merchant to be my true
and lawful Attorney for me and in my name to ask demand sue
for recover and receive all debts and property of what kind
soever which is now due or which may hereafter be due to me
as administratrix aforesaid and on the receipt thereof to grant
discharges for the same to do every other act touching the
premises as well as if I were personally present at the doing
thereof and if necessary to appoint one or more Attorneys
under him hereby ratifying & Confirming all that my said Attorney or his substitute shall lawfully do by virtue hereof IN
WITNESS WHEREOF I have hereunto set my hand & seal
this Seventeenth day of April one thousand eight hundred and
eleven Rachel Heilbron

(L.S. WITNESS Hannah Heilbron* STATE OF NEW
YORK SS on the 22nd day of may 1811 before me came Hannah Heilbron the Subscribing Witness to the within Instrument
to me known who being by me duly sworn made oath that she
saw Rachel Heilbron to her the said Deponent known to be the
same person described in and who executed the within Instrument duly execute the same by signing sealing and delivering
the same and that she the said deponent thereupon subscribed
her name thereto as such Witness of the execution thereof all
which being to me satisfactory evidence of the execution thereof
I allow it to be recorded S COWDREY Master in chy.

## Letter of Administration

The People of the State of New-York By the Grace of God
Free and Independent To Hyam M. Salomon a son of Hyam
Salomon late of the City of Philadelphia, Merchant, deceased
Send Greeting:
Whereas the said Hyam Salomon is alleged, lately died intestate, having whilst living, and at the time of his death, goods,
chattels, or credits within this state . . . [we] do grant unto you
the said Hyam M. Salomon full power by these presents, to administer and faithfully dispose of all and singular the said
goods, chattels, and credits . . . [an inventory]** so made to exhibit . . . into the office of the Surrogate of the said County of
New York, at or before the expiration of six calendar months

---

*Apparently David's sister.
**An inventory was filed but the Surrogate's Court no longer keeps records
which date back that far.

from the date hereof . . . [we] appoint you the said Hyam M. Salomon Administrator of all and singular the goods, chattels, and credits which were of the said Hyam Salomon administered by Rachel Salomon, Eleazer Levi, James Stewart, William Constable and Alexander Robertson, now also deceased . . .

Witness James Campell Surrogate
May 30, 1821

## Court Cases

### Jacob Mordecai

Mordecai had a note for £3,000 NY currency, signed by Salomon and dated December 1, 1784, "for divers goods wares and merchandizes." The New York administrators for Salomon's estate—Eleazer Levy, Alexander Robertson, William Constable and James Stewart, merchants—maintained that they had paid Mordecai. Mordecai sued anyway in the state Supreme Court. A jury was repeatedly called without success. On April 3, 1789, Mordecai did not appear in court, thereby defaulting. The administrators were awarded costs and charges of £21.1.9 in a judgment signed June 13, 1789.

Mordecai also sued Salomon's associate, William Vanderlockt, on the basis of a note for £4,000 NY currency, dated June 4, 1785:

> City and County of New York Jacob Mordecai puts in his place Brockholst Livingston his Attorney against William Van derLockt in a plea of Debt—City and County of New York and the said William Vanderlockt puts in his place James Giles his Attorney at the suit of the said Jacob Mordecai in the plea aforesaid—
> City and County of New York—Be it Remembered that on the last Tuesday in July in this same term before the people of the state of New York in their Supreme Court of Judicature at the City of Albany came Jacob Mordecai by Brockholst Livingston his Attorney and brought here into the Court of the said People their there his certain bill against William VanderLockt being in Custody and of a plea of Debt and there are pledges of Prosecuting to wit John Doe and Richard Roe—which said bill follows in these words "City and County of New York Jacob Mordecai complains of William Vanderlockt being in Custody and of a plea that he tender to the said Jacob four thousand Pounds lawfull money of New York which the said William owes to the said Jacob and unjustly detains from him, for this to wit, that whereas the said William on the fourth day of June

in the Year of our Lord One thousand Seven hundred and Eighty five at the City of New York, to wit, at the westward of the said City and in the County aforesaid by his Certain Writing obligatory Sealed with the Seal of the said William and to the Court of the people of the State of New York now here shewn the date whereof is on the same day and year acknowledged himself to be held and firmly bound to the said Jacob in the said four thousand Pounds to be paid to the said Jacob when he the said William should be thereunto required Nevertheless the said William altho often required he hath not yet paid the said four thousand pounds to the said Jacob but hitherto hath refused and still doth refuse to pay the same to him to the Damage of him the said Jacob twenty pounds And there of he brings Suit Ye — And the said William VanderLockt by James Giles, his Attorney comes and defends the force and Injury when Ye and Says that he cannot deny the action of the said Jacob Mordecai nor that the waiting obligatory is the Deed of him the said William nor that he detains from the said Jacob the said sum of four thousand Dollars against him — Therefore it is considered that the said Jacob recover against the said William his said Debt and also Eight pounds and Six pence — for his damages which he has sustained as well by occasion of the detention of that debt as for his Costs and Charges by him about his suit in His behalf expended to the said Jacob by the Court of the said people now here adjudged by his assent [?] and the said William in Mercy —

Judgment Signed
September. . . .1785
*Richard Morris*

Filed September 13, 1785 of the term of July in the year of our Lord one thousand seven hundred and Eighty-five
Witness Richard Morris Esquire Chief Justice —
M$^C$Kesson —

## Abraham Skinner

On January 1, 1783, Salomon loaned £800 NY currency to Abraham Skinner, "one of the Attornies of the Supreme Court of Judicature for the State of New York." In July, 1786, Aaron Burr, attorney for Salomon's administrators, filed in Supreme Court against Skinner. The jury found for the administrators and the chief justice, Richard Morris, ordered the sheriff to estimate damages. £25.17.16 was added as cost and charges, and £285.17.6 as damages. This final judgment was made by Jonathen Sloss Hobart, November 11, 1786. Skinner did not pay, and the case was brought to the Court for the Correction of Errors on February 19, 1787. The court issued a writ of error. Skinner responded by defaulting, and the administrators could collect only £28.15.5. A few years later, Skinner reached an agreement with Eleazer Levy for a further and final payment and, on August 19, 1805, Levy filed a letter of satisfaction with the Supreme Court.

**Lyon Hart**

The third Tuesday in January, 1786, "Alexander Robertson, William Constable, James Steward and Eleazer Levy administrators of . . . Haym Salomon Deceased at the time of his Death who died Intestate put in their place Aaron Burr their attorney against Lyon Hart in a Plea of Trespass on the Case." Hart owed Salomon's estate £1,800. All told, he was in debt to a number of people for £20,000. On August 2, 1785, Salomon's administrators had said they would settle for £1,600. Hart said he was broke. The case went to the Supreme Court on the third Tuesday of October, 1785: "Whereas the said Lyon Hart on the Second day of May in the year of our lord one thousand seven hundred and eighty three at the City of New York in the Northward of the said City was indebted to the said Haym Salomon in his life time in one thousand Pounds of lawful money of the State of New York for diverse goods wares and Merchandizes by the said Haym Salomon in his life time before that time Sold and delivered to the said Lyon Hart and at his special instance and request and being so indebted he the said Lyon Hart in consideration thereof afterwards to wit" promised Salomon that he would pay back the money when requested. The £800 was mentioned further on in the document. The court found for the administrators and granted a writ of venire.

Hart's lawyer, Brockholst Livingston, filed this with the Supreme Court, March 16, 1786:

> Know all men by those presents That I Lion Hart of the City of New York Merchant am held and firmly bound unto John Osthoudt and John Dumont under the firm of Osthoudt & Dumont, Samuel Mirian Adam Gilchrist, Junior, Nicholas Daniel DuBey and Frederick Devoux under the Firm of DuBey and Company, Peter MacDougall, Jacob Farley and George Barnwall under the firm of Farley and Barnwall, David Galbreath, John Ellis, Samuel Corp, Francis Durand, Peter Landay, Alexander Riddle, Jacob Mordecai, John McCrea for the

*Appendix*

Administrators of Haim Salomon, James Montaudevoh, George Pollock, John Rilson and Stephen N. Bayard under the firm of Ritson and Bayard, Frederick Jay Frederick Cockle & Josiah Ellis of the Cities of New York and Philadelphia Merchants, Richard Platt of the City of New York Broker, and Brockholst Livingston of said City Esquire in the penal sum of Twenty thousand pounds Current money of New York to be paid unto the said [above names repeated] for which payment well and truly to be made I bind myself, my Heirs Executors and Administrators firmly by these presents, Sealed with my Seal dated this Sixteenth day of March in the year of our Lord one thousand Seven hundred and eighty six.

So Hart owed money to his lawyer and Mordecai, too. John McCrea was a lawyer and probably unrelated to the McCrea who had clerked for Salomon; the name was a common one.

### William Rhinelander

Rhinelander held the mortgage on No. 22 Wall Street. Rhinelander did not sue the administrators but instead sued Rachel, as co-signer of the note, her children and her new husband. The curiosity was the drawing in of the children and the following petition wherein Rhinelander wishes the appointment of a guardian so that the children will answer to the complaint. Rhinelander refers to the children as being divided up between Philadelphia and New York. At this time, Ezekiel was thirteen, Deborah eleven, Sarah nine, and Haym M. six.

In Chancery — W Rhinelander     *Petition*
                                Bogert

Filed 9 Aug$^t$ 1791
William Rhinelander
          vs
David Halbrun and          To the Honorable Robert R.
Rachel his wife Hesikiah    Livingston Esquire Chancellor
Solomon Haym Solomon          of the State of New York —
Deborah Solomon and            The petition of William
Sarah Solomon . . .     Rhinelander the above Complainant

Humbly Sheweth —
That your petition lately obtained a commission out of this honorable Court in the above cause — appointing commissioners in Philadelphia to assign a gaurdian to the four last above named defendants for the purpose of taking their answer by such guardian — That your petitioner has since discovered that some of the said defendants reside in the City of New

York — He therefore prays that your Honor will direct a commission to be issued to Andrew Vantiujle [?], Andrew Stockholm and Gilbert C. Willet as commissioners to assign a guardian to such of the defendants as are infants and reside in the City of New York for the purpose of taking their answer by such guardian and that the said commissioners or any two of them may execute the said commission —

July 23 1791

And your Petitioner —
shall pray &c,
Will<sup>m</sup> Rhinelander

*Let the petition be granted*
*RRL*

Rhinelander was given a writ of venditioni exponas, which meant that the house and property could be seized and sold.

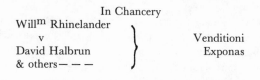

In Chancery

Will<sup>m</sup> Rhinelander
v
David Halbrun
& others — — —

Venditioni
Exponas

Bogert
Filed 22 Dec<sup>m</sup> 1791

The People of the State of New York to our Sheriff of our City and County of New York greeting whereas William Rhinelander lately exhibited his bill of complaint in our Court of Chancery against David Halbrun and Rachel his wife Ezekiel Solomon Haym Solomon, Deborah Solomon and Sarah Solomon and therein prayed the slale of the following premises to wit, All that certain Messuage* or dwelling house and lot of ground thereunto belonging situate lying and being in the second (formerly called the East) Ward of the City of New York and now in the tenure and occupation of Anthony Bleecker containing in breadth (including the Alley) in the front to Wall Street forty four feet two inches and in the rear to the ground formerly owned by Samuel Payton (including the Alley) fifty feet and one inch and in length on the Northwest side to the house and ground formerly of Peter Adalph fifty one feet six inches and on the Southeasterly side to the ground

---

*Messuage: the portion of land actually occupied; the building.

formerly owned by Francis Child fifty feet seven Inches the premisses hereby intended to be granted were formerly held by Francis Lucas and the house is now called number two in Wall street together with the buildings and appurtenances thereunto belonging, which said premisses were charged, in the complainants said bill to have been mortgaged to him by Haym Solomon, deceased, and the said Rachel Halbrun, in the life time of the said Haym Solomon and during his coverture with the said Rachel. And Whereas such proceedings was thereupon had in our said Court of Chancery that it was adjudged and decreed by the same Court that the above described premisses should be sold at public vendue by our Sheriff aforesaid as by the record of the said proceedings and the decree aforesaid manifestly appears to us, Wherefore we command and strictly enjoin you that you make sale of the said mortgaged premisses above described with the appurtenances at public vendue first causing an advertisement or notice of such intended sale to be inserted in one or more of the publick newspapers printed in this State and continuing the same in such paper or papers weekly for six weeks before the day to be by you appointed for the sale of the said premisses. And we further command and strictly enjoin you, that at the day so by you appointed and notified you proceed to sell the same to the highest bidder. And that you return the monies arrising by the Sale of the said premisses into our said Court of Chancery on the fourteenth day of January next wheresoever it shall then be with this writ, Witness Robert R. Livingston Esquire our Chancellor at Clermont in the County of Columbia the seventh day of October in the year of our Lord one thousand and seven hundred and ninety one — — —

William Rhinelander     {
in proper person                               Cooper    Clerk

The sheriff was Marinus Willet. He had been commissioned in early 1784, according to the *Mayor's Court Minutes, Feb. 10, 1784 to Sept. 21, 1785*, p. 3. In early 1786, he had been given the Supreme Court writ of venire against Abraham Skinner in the case Burr handled for Salomon's administrators. Willet had taken no action against Skinner. This time, Willet followed the court order and ran this ad in *The Daily Advertiser* for six weeks, beginning October 15, 1791:

Sheriffs Sales,
By virtue of a writ of venditioni exponas to me directed, issued out of the honorable Court of Chancery of this state, will be sold at public vendue, at the merchants Coffee-house in the City of New-York, on the first day of December next, at

133

> twelve o'clock in the forenoon . . . all that certain messuage or
> dwelling house and lot of ground thereunto belonging, situate
> . . . in the second . . . ward . . . and now in the tenure and oc-
> cupation of Anthony Bleecker . . . the house is now called
> number twenty-two in Wall-street . . .
>
> Oct. 15                                              M. WILLET
>                                                           Sheriff

In late 1787, Rhinelander had had Mordecai ejected from the
house and Bleecker, as he had done before Salomon bought it, moved
in. A.L. Bleecker & Sons sold dry goods, hops, Madiera, tea and land.
The house was bought at auction by John Broome, alderman in 1785,
partner in Broome, Platt & Co. of No. 190 Water Street; John
Delafield, a broker and auctionier at No. 5 Queen Street who sold
Negroes, goods, land and who, in 1784, had "wanted Bills drawn by
the Hon. Robert Morris, or J. Swanwick, Esq.; either those that are
due, or those date in July, August, September, October, or
November"; William Laight, who was campaigning for Third Ward
alderman; and Guilian Ver Planck and John Watts, merchants. Their
bid was £2,510. Willet filed the notice of sale with the court.

> I Marinus Willet Sheriff of the City and County of New
> York do hereby certify that in obedience to the within writ I ex-
> posed the premises within described to sale on the first day of
> December instant that being the day appointed by me for the
> sale thereof and that the same were sold for two thousand five
> hundred and ten pounds that being the highest sum bid for the
> same and I further certify that I have the said sum now in my
> hands which I received from John Broome, Gulian Ver Planck,
> John Delafield, John Watts and William Laight—dated this
> 20th day of December 1791
>
>                                       M. Willet    Sheriff

Rhinelander was then ordered to give an accounting of the mortgage, taxes, rents, etc. pertaining to the property.

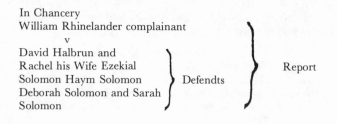

In Chancery
William Rhinelander complainant
               v
David Halbrun and
Rachel his Wife Ezekial      ⎫
Solomon Haym Solomon         ⎬  Defendts        Report
Deborah Solomon and Sarah    ⎭
Solomon

In Pursuance of a Decree of the Honorable Court of Chancery that the above Complainant should account on Oath before one of the Masters of the said Court touching all Monies received by him as Payments on the Mortgaged Premisses mentioned in the Bill of Complaints of the said Complainant and touching all Rents and Profits thereof received by him and touching all Monies for Repairs Taxes or otherwise expended by him in and about the same, and also that the mortgage and Bonds mentioned in the said Bill of Complaint should be exhibited to are of the said Masters and that the said Complainant should likewise account on Oath touching the Amount of the Principal and Interest due thereon and that he should tax the said Complainants Bill of Costs and report the Amount thereof together with the said Principal and Interest. I the undersigned have been attended by William Rhinelander the above Complainant who on Oath duly administered by me to him did duly account pursuant to the Tenor and affect of the said Decree: and I do thereupon Report that the amount of the monies due on the Mortgage Premisses aforesaid for Principal and Interest and the monies expended by him for Repairs Taxes or otherwise in and about the said Premisses, is three thousand six hundred and sixty two Pounds ten Shillings and three Pence, that the Amount of the Monies received by him as Payments thereon and Rents and Profits is One thousand seven hundred and ninety Pounds three Shillings and one Penny and that deducting the said amount of Payments Rents and Profits from the said Amount of Monies for Principal and Interest and the Monies expended for Repairs Taxes or otherwise, there remains a Balance due to the said William Rhinelander of One thousand Eight hundred and sevent two Pounds one Shillings and two Pence, all which appears by the Account Current hereunto annexed and I do also Report that I have taxed the Complainants Costs which amount to eighty nine Pounds . . . and nine pence all which is submitted to the said Honorable Court by

James M Hughes
Master in Chancery

Dated this 14 December 1791

Enclosed was a document handwritten by Rhinelander. It was titled, "The Mortgag'd premisses of Haym Solomons in account Current with William Rhinelander." The first side read:

1784
feby 21    To your Bond of the date payable
       1 May                                   £1200..

|  |  |  |  |
|---|---|---|---|
|  | To Interest till first of May | 37.6.8 | 1237..6.8. |
| May 1 | To charge of pritost (?) of your draft on Daniel Parker & Co. for said Sum | 1.4-- |  |
|  | Interest due from 1 to 19th May | 4.6.7 | 5..10.7 |

|  |  |  |  |
|---|---|---|---|
| 1788 feby 1 | To Colonel Hamilton & Sheriffs Bills for Ejectment |  | 11..7..-- |
|  | To Cash paid Taxes due for 1787 |  | 6..6..8 |
| May 14 | To Cash paid Taxes Repairs for 1788 |  | 23..9..10 |

|  |  |  |  |
|---|---|---|---|
| 1789 Jany 6 | To Cash Paid Taxes Repairs for 1789 |  | 15..15.1 |

|  |  |  |  |
|---|---|---|---|
| 1791 feby 9 | To Cash paid Taxes Repairs for 1790 |  | 10.14.8 |
| June 3 | To Cash paid Taxes Repairs for 1791 |  | 29..3.9 |
|  | To Second Bond date feby 21 1784 | £1500 |  |
|  | To interest due on the above to 21 decem 1791 is 7 years & 10 months } | 822.10 |  |
|  |  |  | 2322.10 |
|  |  |  | £3662.. 4..3 |

The next side read:

|  |  |  |
|---|---|---|
| 1784 feby 21 | By draft on Daniel Parker & Co. | 1237.6.8 |
| 1788 feby 1 | By Cash received on account of house rent | 40..— — |
| June 6 | By Cash "                    " | 40..— — |
| Sept 15 | By Cash "                    " | 40..— — |
| Nov 25 | By Cash "                    " | 40..— — |

136

| 1789 | | | | |
|---|---|---|---|---|
| June 24 | By Cash received | | | 80.. — — |
| Nov 6 | By Cash | " | " | 40.. — — |
| Decem$^r$ | | | | |
| 1 | By Cash | " | " | 40.. — — |

| 1790 | | | | |
|---|---|---|---|---|
| May 29 | By Cash | " | " | 79.. 9.. 9 |

| 1791 | | | | |
|---|---|---|---|---|
| May 26 | By Cash | " | " | 60.. — — |
| Aug 6 | By Cash | " | " | 40.. — — |
| Nov 30 | By Cash | " | " | 40.. — — |
| Decem 1 | By Cash | " | " | 13.. 6.. 8 |
| | balance due W$^m$ Rhinelander | | | 1872..1..2 |

£3662..4..3

New York December 21   1791
Errors Excepted
W$^m$ Rhinelander

## *No. 22 Wall Street*

Indentures were not filed for another three years. They incorrectly give the date of the bonds as October 21, 1784, instead of February. This was because the Surrogate's Court had its files hand-copied in 1873, and a number of clerical errors were made. The original documents were then either lost or destroyed.

The new owners of the property achieved a better deal than they probably expected. By 1806, Wall Street was crowded with financial institutions: U.S. Bank, branch (38 Wall Street), Manhattan Bank (23), Merchant's Bank (25), New York Bank (32); insurance companies at numbers 23, 34, 44, 49, 50, 59 and 66; and two Offices of Exchange for Notes (Samuel Beebee at No. 55 and Benjamin Butler at No. 35). City Hall was on Wall Street, opposite Broad. As John

Low described it, "Wall-Street ... begins in Broad-way, opposite Trinity Church, crossing New, Nassau, Broad, and William, & Pearl-st. ends at Coffee-house-slip, 1st Ward. In this street are all the Banks."

Recorded for and at the
Request of Mr. John Broome
and others this 8th day of
March 1794

    This Indenture made the first day of December in the Year of our Lord one thousand Seven hundred and ninety one Between Marinus Willet Esquire Sheriff of the City and County of New York of the one part and John Broome Guilian Ver Planck John Watts John Delafield and William Laight of the Said City Merchants of the other part whereas William Rhinelander of the said City lately exhibited his bill of Complaint in the Court of Chancery of the State against David Halburn and Rachel his wife Ezekiel Solomon Deborah Solomon Haym Solomon and Sarah Solomon Praying the Sale of All that certain messuage and Dwelling house and lot of Ground thereunto belonging Situate lying and being in the Second Ward formerly the East Ward of the Said City of New York and now in the tenure and occupation of Anthony Bleecker Containing in breadth (including the Ally) in front to Wall Street forty four feet two inches and in the Rear to the ground formerly owned by Samuel Payton (including the Ally) fifty feet and one inch and in length on the north west side to the house and ground formerly of Peter Adalph fifty one feet six inches and in the Southeasterly Side to the Ground formerly owned by Francis Child fifty feet seven inches the premisses hereby intended to be granted were formerly held by Rancis Lucas and the house is now called Number twenty two in Wall Street Together with all and Singular the Buildings passages lights Easements and all other privileges and profits commodities emoluments hereditaments and appurtenances whatsoever to the Said Messuage or Dwelling house and Lot of Ground and premises of any part thereof belonging or any wise appertaining or which then were or formerly had been accepted reparted taken or enjoyed to or with the Same or as part parcels or member thereof for any part there of and the reversion and reversions remainder and remainders rents Issues of all and Singular the Said Premises and of every part and parcel thereof with their and every of their appurtenances And Also all the Estate right title and In-

terest property possession claim and demand of him of him the
Said Haym Solomon and Rachel his wife of in and to all and
Singular the Said premisses and of in and to every part and
parcel thereof with the appurtenances excepting and always
reserving unto the Said Owners and Possession of the Lot of
Ground formerly owned by the Said Samuel Payton free leave
and liberty to pass and repass in and through the way or ally
lying north the house and ground formerly belonging to the
Said Peter Adalph at all convenient time in the day only and
also the like liberty to Peter Degrove or if the owners and
possessors of the house formerly belonging to the Said Peter if
they have any Such sight to the Same under the hand and Seal
of Thomas Clark late of the City of New York Merchant and
not otherwise which premisses above described were charged in
the Said Bills to have been Mortgaged to the Said William
Rhinelander by Haym Solomon late of Philadelphia in the
State of Pennsylvania Merchant deceased and by the Said
Rachel Halbrun before her Marriage with the above named
David Halbrun and during her Coverture with the Said Haym
Solomon deceased for the purpose of Securing the payment of
two Bonds one of which was in the Penal Sum of two thousand
four hundred pounds Conditioned for the payment of one thousand two hundred and the other in the penal sum of Three
Thousand Pounds conditioned for the payment of one thousand five hundred pounds with Interest on the Said Several
Sums And Whereas such proceedings were there upon had in
the Said Court of Chancery that it was ordered and Decreed
among other things that a writ of vendition exponas Should
Issue under the Seal of the Said Court directed to the Sheriff
of the City and County of New York Commanding him to
make Sale at public vendue of the premisses Mortgaged in and
by the above mentioned mortgage and that the Said Sheriff
Should cause an advertisement or notice of such Sale so intended to be made by him to be inserted in one or more of the
Public News Papers printed in this State and to Continue the
Same in the Said paper or papers weekly for Six weeks Suc-
cessively before the day to be appointed by him for the Said Sale
as by the Record of the Said Proceedings and the Decree of the
Said Court of Chancery remaining in the office of the Register
of the Said Court may appear reference being thereunto had
And Whereas the Said Marinus Willet Sheriff of the Said City
and County of New York pursuant to the Said writ of Vendition exponas issued out of the Said Court of Chancery upon the
order and Decrees aforesaid did Conformably thereto cause
an advertisement or notice of such Sale to be advertised in one
of the Public News Papers printed in the State of New York (to

wit in the News papers Printed by Francis Child and John
Swain of the City of New York public printers) for the Spase
of Six weeks . . . And where as the Said Marinus Willet Esquire
did on the first day of December in the Said year one thousand
seven hundred and ninety one being the the day appointed by
him in the Said Advertisement for the Sale of the Said Mortgaged Premises by virtue of the Said writ of Venditions exponas offer the Said Mortgaged premises for Sale at public
Vendue at the Merchants Coffee house . . . and the same was
struck off to the Said parties of the Second part for the Sum of
two thousand five hundred and ten pounds that being the
highest Sum bid for the Same and which Sum was bid by the
Said parties of the Second part as by the Said writ of Venditions
exponas and the return thereof enclosed by the Said Marinus
Willet Esquire filed in the office of the Register of the Said
Court may appear Now therefore this Indenture witnesseth
that the Said Marinus Willet Esquire Sheriff of the City and
County of New York by virtue of the Said writ of the Act in
such case made and provided for and in Consideration of the
Said Sum of two thousand five hundred and ten pounds to him
in hand paid by the Said parties of the Second part at or before
the ensealing and delivery of these presents the receipt whereof
is hereby acknowledged and the Said parties on the Second part
therefrom forever hereby released Hath Granted Bargained
Sold aliened released enfeoffed* conveyed and confirmed and
by these presents Doth grant bargain sell alien release enfeoff
convey and confirm unto the Said parties of the Second part
and to their heirs and assigns for ever All that the Said
Messuage Dwelling house lot of ground and premises herein
before particularly described and recited And Also all the
Estate right title interest property claim and demand in law and
equity of him the Said Marinus Willet Esquire Sheriff as
aforesaid by virtue of the Said Decree and of the Said writ and
also all the Estate right title Interest claim and Demand in Law
and Equity which the said Haym Solomon deceased had on the
Said premises as also all the Interest and title of the Said defen-
dant in the Said Suit in Chancery and each of their of in and
to the Same And the Reversion and Reversions Remainder and
Remainders Rents Issues and profits of the Said premises with
the Appurtenances To have and to hold the Said Messuage
dwelling house lot of grounds and premises with the
hereditaments and appurtenances unto the Said John Broome
Gulian Ver Planck John Watts John Delafield and William
Laight their heirs and assigns to the only use and behoof of the

---

*Enfeoff: to put someone in possession of property.

said John Broome Gulian Ver Planck John Watts John
Delafield and William Laight their heirs and assigns for ever as
joint tenants and not as tenants in Common In Witness
whereof the parties to these Presents have hereunto Inter-
changeably Set their hands and Seals the day and year first
above written Marinus Willet Sheriff Sealed and delivered in
the presence of the word "pounds" interlined in the fifteenth line
between the words "hundred" and "with" the words "notice of"
interlined on the twenty first line between the words "or" and
"Such" the word "thousand" interlined on the twenty fourth line
between the words "two" and "five" the word "Second" written
on an erazure in the Seventh line from the bottom between the
words "presents" and "Grant" Corns J. Bogert James DeLap-
Laine Received on the Day and year first written mentioned
from the parties of the Second part within named the Sum of
two thousand five hundred and ten pounds being the full consideration money within expressed M Willet Witness Corns J.
Bogert James K. Delaplaine Be it Remembered that on the
twenty-first day of December in the Year of our Lord one thousand Seven hundred and ninety one Personally appeared
before me John Sloss Hobart one of the Justices of the Supreme
Court of the State of New York the within named Marinus
Willet Esquire who acknowledged that he sealed and delivered
the within Indenture as his Voluntary Act and Deed for the
uses within mentioned And I having examined the Same and
finding no erazures Interlineations there in but those noted do
allow the same to be recorded
Jn Sloss Hobart

Recorded for and at the<br>
Request of M<sup>r</sup> John Broome<br>
and others this 10<sup>th</sup> day<br>
of March 1794

This Indenture made the twenty eighth day of December
in the year of our Lord one thousand Seven hundred and ninety
one between William Rhinelander of the City of New York
Merchant of the one part and John Broome Gulian Ver Planck
John Watts John Delafield and William Laight of the Said City
Merchants of the other part Whereas Haym Solomon late of
Philadelphia in the State of Pennsylvania Merchant indebted
to the Said William Rhinelander in two bonds bearing date
respectively the twenty first day of October in the year of our
Lord one thousand Seven hundred and Eighty four one of
which was in the Penal Sum of two thousand four hundred
Pounds Conditioned for the payment one thousand two hund-
red pounds and the other in the Penal Sum of Three thousand

pound Conditioned for the payment of one thousand five hundred pounds with the lawful Intent for the Same did together with his wife Rachel for the purpose of Securing the payment of the Sums mentioned in the Condition of the Said two Several bonds by Indenture of Lease and Release bearing date the twentieth of October in the year of our Lord one thousand Seven hundred and Eighty four and the Release the day after Release and convey to the Said William Rhinelander and to his heir and assigns forever All that certain Messuage or Dwelling house and Lot of Ground thereunto belonging situate lying and being in the Second Ward (formerly the East Ward) of the Said City of New York and now in the tenure and occupation of Anthony Bleecker Containing in breadth (including the alley) in ... etc ... And the Reversion ... And also all the Estate right title Enterest property possession claim and Demand of him the Said Haym and Rachel his wife of in and to all and Singular the said premisses ... To have and to hold the said premisses to the said William Rhinelander his heirs and assigns to the only use and behoof of the Said William Rhinelander his heirs and assigns forever Subject Nevertheless to a proviso therein contained that the Indentures of Lease and Release before recited should be void on the Payment of the Several Sums mentioned in the Condition in the Said Bonds with the Interest on the days and at the times therein respectively mentioned And Whereas the Said Haym Solomon afterwards departed this life intestate leaving at his Death four Children to wit Ezekiel Solomon Haym Solomon Deborah Solomon and Sarah Solomon and also the said Rachel his Widow who afterwards intermarried with one David Halbrun And Whereas the Said William Rhinelander did file his bill of Complaint in the Court of Chancery of this State upon the Said Mortgage against the Said David Halbrun and Rachel his wife and the Said four Children of the Said Haym Solomon deceased and obtained a Decree that the Said Premisses Should be Sold by the Sheriff ... at public Vendue And Whereas the Said premisses were accordingly Sold ... in the first Day of December ... to the Said parties of the Second part for the sum of [£2,510] ... Now therefore this Indenture Witnesseth that the Said William Rhinelander for and in Consideration of the Sum of [illegible] Shillings to him in paid by the Said parties of the Second part at or before the Ensealing and delivery hereof the receipt whereof is hereby acknowledged Hath bargained Sold Released Enfeoffed and Confirmed and by these presents Doth Grant bargain sell Release Enfeoff and Confirm unto the Said parties of the Second part the above described mortgaged premisses with the hereditaments and appurtenances and all his right title and Interest Claim and Demand in Law and Equity of in and to the Same And the Reversion and Reversions Remainder and Remainders Rents Issues and profits thereof To have and to hold the Said premises mentioned in the Said Mortgage unto the Said John Broome Gulian Ver Planck John Watts John Delafield and William Laight their heirs and assigns to the only use and behoof of the Said John Broome Gulian Ver Planck John Watts John Delafield and William Laight their heirs and assigns forever as joint tenants and not as Tenants in Common Provided Always and these presents are upon the express condition that nothing herein Contained Shall be deemed or taken to amount to a Covenant on the part of the Said William Rhinelander to Warrant or Defend the Said Mortgaged premises to the Said Granters above named but Shall only operate as a Release of all such Right title and Interest whatsoever which he the Said William Rhinelander now has or which his heirs or Executors may or can hereafter have of in and to the Said premises . . . (William Rhinelander seals; interline changes) . . .

Witness Cornelius J. Bogert Received
        Feb. 2, 1792
Recorded James M. Hughes a Master in Chancery

## Tax Lists

The following tax lists do not give a totally accurate representation of a person's wealth, since they are only for the Philadelphia area and are based on diverse methods of assessment. The best way to use them is as a comparative measure between people — and not between years. The taxes differed from year to year, as did the assessments.

1769 and 1779 are from the *Pennsylvania Archives*, vol. 14, pp. 41, 172, 486–529. 1780 has been given previously. 1781 is from *Ibid*, vol. 15, pp. 583–745. 1782 and 1783 are from *Ibid*, vol. 16, pp. 138–817. Money is in Pennsylvania currency.

**1769**

| Name | Acres | Horses | Cattle | Servants | Tax |
|---|---|---|---|---|---|
| *Frankford and New Hanover Townships* | | | | | |
|   M. Hillegass | 130 | 2 | 2 | | 12.10.8 |
| *Dock Ward* | | | | | |
|   Thomas Fitzsimons | | 1 | | 2 | 8.13.4 |

**1779**  A proprietary tax, assessed May 26 based on the tax law passed 1777, 5 shillings per 1 plus 30 shillings per head.

| Name | Tax |
|------|-----|
| Thomas Willing | 966 |
| John Chaloner | 15 |
| Heyman Levy | 10 |
| M. Hillegass | 230 |

**1781** Assessment August 23.

| Name | Valuation | Tax |
|------|-----------|-----|
| Benjamin Seixas | 642 | 6.18.1 |
| Simon Nathan | 126 | 1. 7.1 |
| Hannah Levy | | |
|     For Benj'n Francklin's est. | 100 | 1. 3.0 |
| Abraham Levy | 50 | 0.10.9 |
| Ezekiah Levy | — — | 6. 0.0 |
| Michael Gratz | 490 | 5. 5.5 |
| Eleazer Levy | 100 | 1. 3.0 |
| John Holker | 3,000 | 34.10.0 |
| Solomon Myers Cohen | 485 | 4.12.0 |
| Isaac Moses | 2,904 | 33. 7.11 |
| Haym Solomon | 172 | 2. 4.7 |
| John Chaloner | 164 | 1.17.7 |
| Robert Morris | 3,500 | 40. 5.0 |
| Robert Morris | 8,764 | 87.12.10 |
| William Turnball & Co. | 14,500 | 166.15.0 |
| Sam'l Ingles & Co. | 1,700 | 19.11.0 |
|     for 2 ships and 2 brigs | 3,870 | — — |
| **1782** Moses Nathan | 855 | 5.17.8 |
| James McCrea | 407 | 2. 6.6 |
| Mr. McCrea | — — | 1. 0.0 |
| Robert Morris | 2,500 | 13.17.1 |
| John Ross & Co. | 4,805 | 26.12.7 |
| John Ross | 1,484 | 8. 4.6 |
| Wm Bingham | 5,361 | 29.14.1 |
| Isaac Moses | 920 | 5. 2.0 |
| Moses Cohen | 362 | 1.18.7 |
| Haym Solomon | 64 | 6.4 |
| Hyam Solomon | 225 | 1. 4.9 |
| Hyams Solomon's | 105 | 11.1 |
| Hyams Solomon's est. | 171 | .18.2 |
| Hyam Solomon | 280 | 1.15.11 |

# *Appendix*

**1783**

| Name | Acres | Horses | Cattle | Sheep | Negroes |
|---|---|---|---|---|---|
| Arthur St. Clair | | 3 | 1 | | |
| John Nixon, mercht | | | 1 | | 2 |
| John Ross, mercht | | 2 | 1 | | |
| Samuel Ingles, mercht | | 2 | | | 1 |
| Edward Shippen | | 1 | 1 | | 2 |
| Andrew Hamilton | | 2 | 1 | | 2 |
| John Chaloner, mercht | | 1 | | | 1 |
| Tench Francis | | 1 | | | 2 |
| James Wilson | | 2 | 1 | | 3 |
| Robert Morris | | 7 | 2 | | 1 |
| John Swanwick | | | 1 | | 3 |
| Jonas Philips, mercht | | | 1 | | 2 |
| Isaac Moses, mercht | | 1 | | | 1 |
| | | | | | |
| *Moyamensing Township* | | | | | |
|     Robert Morris' est. | 4 | | | | |
|     Thomas Willing's est. | 15½ | | | | |
| | | | | | |
| *Moreland Township* | | | | | |
|     James Wilson | | 2 | 4 | | |
| | | | | | |
| *New Hanover Township* | | | | | |
|     David Frank's est. | 60 | | | | |
| | | | | | |
| *Oxford Township* | | | | | |
|     Thomas Willing's est. | 173 | | | | |
| | | | | | |
| *Passyunk Township* | | | | | |
|     Michael Hillegass's est. | 27 | | | | |
|     Edward Shippen's est. | 8½ | | | | |
| | | | | | |
| *Providence Township* | | | | | |
|     Israel Jacobs | 130 | 4 | 4 | 10 | |

# Notes

## I. The Revolution Begins

1. The terms Whig and Tory were first used during the 1679 debate over whether to exclude the Catholic James, Duke of York, from the succession to the British throne. The Whigs were Calvinists and believed in the concept of a "contract" between ruler and subjects. Their leader was George Savile, Marquis of Halifax. Opposing him was the Earl of Danby, former minister to King Charles, and a believer in the divine succession of Stuarts. His Tory party was composed of Anglican gentry. After William of Orange deposed King James II in 1688, he and Princess Mary were given joint rule over Britain through an act of the Whig dominated Parliament. William later sided with the Tories. In America, as in England, Whigs were those who supported the social compact theory, and Tories were those who supported the monarchy.

2. S.M. Dubnow, *History of the Jews in Russia and Poland* (Philadelphia: 1916), p. 188.

3. In 1391, Spanish Jews were given the choice between conversion and death. Those who converted were called *marranos*, or "swine." There is some controversy over whether marranos remained Jews in secret or actually embraced Christianity. Obviously, it was some of both. Later, marranos gave financial support to Christopher Columbus and a few sailed with him.

4. Louis Lewin, *Geschichte der Juden in Lissa* (Pinne: 1904), p. 130.

147

"Am 4. Februar jenes Jahres traf Alexander Josef v. Sulkowski mit der Gemeinde ein Übereinkommen, laut welchem nach Ablauf der vier Jahre die Gemeinde ihre jährliche Steuer von 15000 Gulden wieder entrichtet und die inzwischen auf 60000 Gulden aufgelaufene Schuld in jährlichen Raten von 10000 Gulden zurückzahlt." ("On February 4 of that year, Alexander Josef v. Sulkowski agreed with the congregation that after a hiatus of four years the congregation would again pay its annual tax of 15,000 gulden and start to pay back the interest accumulated in the interim on the 60,000 gulden in annual installments of 10,000 gulden.")

5. Harold Korn, "Receipt Book of Judah and Moses M. Hays, Commencing January 12, 1763, and Ending July 18, 1776," in *Publications of the American Jewish Historical Society* no. 27 (1920). Alexander Solomons, apparently Haym's brother, also signed the voucher, which was no. 121. In March, 1768, Alexander Solomons was involved in a court case with Robert Stapleton. (*Mayor's Court Minutes, Apr. 30, 1765 to Mar. 1, 1768*, p. 405.) A broker, he eventually moved to Pensacola, Florida.

6. Or, in the words of Rabbi Jacob Emden (1697–1776): "We have not been granted rest among the nations with our humiliation, affliction and homelessness, because this sense of mourning [over Jerusalem] has left our hearts. While being complacent in a land not ours, we have forgotten Jerusalem." Arthur Hertzberg, ed., *Judaism* (New York: 1962), p. 164.

7. The Pentateuch lists 613 commandments which a Jew is to follow. A major tenet is charity. Loans to the poor should be without interest but, when interest is charged, the debtor should not be pressed for payment unless able to pay. Business must be conducted honestly. Maimonides (1135–1204), in his *Mishneh Torah*, listed eight degrees of charity. The best is giving a gift or loan; the next is giving anonymously to charity. He emphasized economic independence. Moses Luzatto (1707–1747), the Italian mystic, wrote in his *Mesillat Yesharim* that "every man, according to his status and how he is looked upon by his contemporaries, must be careful not to do anything which is improper for a man of his standing ... If he does not act in this way, the Name of Heaven is profaned through him." Hertzberg, *Judaism*, p. 68.

8. Figures cited by Edmund Burke in a speech to the House of Commons, March 22, 1775. Cited in Alden T. Vaughan, *Chronicles of the American Revolution* (NY: 1965), pp. 107ff.

9. Isaac Franks may have been one of the prisoners Salomon helped to escape. The two were friends until 1782.

10. The Jewish year is composed of twelve lunar months: Nissan, Iyyar, Sivan, Tammuz, Av, Elul, Tishri, Heshvan, Kislev, Tevet, Shevat and Adar. Each month has 29 or 30 days. The year itself is solar and has 365 days. To reconcile the two, one month is added seven times every nineteen solar years.

# Notes

11. "The Lyons Collection" in *Publications of the American Jewish Historical Society* no. 27, 1920, p. 251.

12. Isaac Pinto translated "Prayers for Shabbath, Rosh-Hashanah, and Kippur, or The Sabbath, the Beginning of the Year, and the Day of Atonements; with the Amidah and Musaph of the Moadim, or Solemn Seasons. According to the Order of the Spanish and Portuguese Jews," printed in New York by John Holt (1766).

13. Disorderliness affected not only Jews. The following appeared in *The Pennsylvania Packet*, Saturday, June 19, 1779:

> The SYNOD of New-York and Philadelphia, taking into consideration the low and declining state of religion and the abounding iniquity amongst us, for which an holy God yet continues to visit our country with his righteous judgments, appoint the fourth Thursday of July to be observed by the Churches under their care, as a Day of Public Fasting and Prayer.

## II. Jews Flee New York

1. The bounties were actually proportionate to time in service and ranks attained. For example, in 1790, Capt. L. Bleeker received 1800 acres, Col. Peter Gansevoort 3000 acres, and Maj. Gen. Alexander McDougall 7200 acres.

2. Vaughan, *Chronicles*, pp. 191ff. The table has been edited.

3. Hertzberg, *Judaism*, p. 69.

## III. Salomon as Broker

1. According to a report to the 31st Congress: "On the accession of the Count de La Luzerne to the embassy from France, Mr. Salomon was made the banker of the government ... He was also appointed by Monsieur Roquebrune, treasurer of the forces of France in America, to the office of their paymaster-general, which he executed free of charge." Madison C. Peters quotes a letter from the Count de Vergennes, France's Foreign Minister, to Ambassador Luzerne stating that in a period of two years, Salomon handled 150,000,000 livre as banker to the government. Peters, *The Jews in America* (NY: 1905), p. 43. One dollar specie equalled 5 livre 8⅓ sous, meaning that Salomon disbursed slightly under $30,000,000 specie. That figure seems extremely high.

2. *The Pennsylvania Archives*, ed. William Henry Egle, series 3, vol. 15 (Harrisburg: 1897), pp. 191–362.

3. *Memoirs of the Marshall Count de Rochambeau* (NY: 1971), pp. 30–32. This is a reprint of the original translation by M.W.E. Wright, published in 1838.

4. Peter Stephen Du Poneceau, *Autobiography*, Sept. 20, 1837, cited in Edwin Wolf and Maxwell Whiteman, *The History of the Jews of Philadelphia* (Philadelphia: 1957), p. 106.

## IV. The Jews of Philadelphia

1. Rendon later wrote to Don Jose Marie de Navarro, the Governor-General of Cuba. "Mr. Salomon has advanced the money for the service of his most Catholic Majesty and I am indebted to his friendship, in this particular, for the support of my character as his most Catholic Majesty's agent here, with any degree of credit and reputation; and without it I should not have been able to render that protection and assistance to his Majesty's subjects that his Majesty enjoins and my duty requires." The loan was never repaid.

2. The Seixases were already part of the Levy family. Their father, Isaac, had married Rachel, daughter of Moses and Grace Levy. So it was a marriage of first cousins when Benjamin married Zipporah. Benjamin had been a saddler in New York and in 1776 was a member of the Fusiliers Co. of the First Battalion of the New York Militia. He went to Connecticut with his brother, then moved to Philadelphia in 1779. He privateered with Isaac Moses and made a great deal of money. He also was a partner with Hayman in the firm Seixas & Levy. As for Gershom, he studied under Joseph Jessurun Pinto when the latter was hazan of Shearith Israel (1759–1765). On July 3, 1768, at the age of 23, he applied for the job of hazan, a position he was granted. His first wife was Elkalah, daughter of Abraham and Sarah Myers Cohen.

3. Frederick William Augustus, the Baron von Steuben, was born in Prussia in 1730. An overweight man with bulging eyes, thick lips and a protruding chin, he was a captain during the Seven Years War and later became a knight of the Order of Fidelity in Baden-Durlach, and was rumored to be a mason. Hearing of the American Revolution, he traveled to Paris and told the American commissioners that he was a great soldier. With letters of reference from Franklin and Deane, he set out with the goal of persuading George Washington that he was a great soldier. In May, 1778, Congress appointed him inspector general of the army, with the rank of major general. Steuben trained the army while trying to convince people that he should be given a couple of regiments of his own. He was finally made a division commander for the battle of Yorktown.

4. Quoting a letter to the congregation in the West Indies. Congregations strove to help each other. New York gave money to Newport for the building of that synagogue. In 1770, Philadelphia Jews gave £13.10.0, New York Jews £32.1.6, and Newport £25.12.0 to the congregation of Hebron in Palestine. In 1773, members of Shearith Israel gave £38.10.6 to Jews living in St. Eustatius, a Dutch island, to help rebuild a temple destroyed in a hurricane.

5. It is possible that Morris was referring to military certificates, which were also known as Pierce's notes. It is generally assumed that these notes were not issued until early 1784.

## V. The Revolution Winds Down

1. In 1768, Rebecca's sister Abigail married the wealthy gentleman Andrew Hamilton of Philadelphia. According to tax records, Hamilton owned two horses, one cow and two slaves in 1783. *Pennsylvania Archives*, vol. 16, p. 780. Abigail and Rebecca loved social life and gossip. On August 10, 1781, Rebecca wrote her sister from New York: "By and by, few New York ladies know how to entertain company in their own houses unless they introduce card tables except this family . . . I don't know a woman or girl that can chat above half an hour, and that on the form of a cap, the colour of a ribbon or the set of a hoop-stay or jupon. I will do our ladies, that is Philadelphians, the justice to say they have more cleverness in the turn of an eye than the NY girls have in their whole composition . . . Here, or more properly speaking in NY, you enter the room with a formal set curtesy and after the how do's, 't is a fine, or a bad day, and those trifling nothings are finish'd, all's a dead call 'till the cards are introduced . . . The misses, if they have a favourite swain, frequently decline playing for the pleasure of making love — for to all appearances 'tis the ladies and not the gentlemen, that shew a preference nowadays . . ." Lee M. Friedman, *Jewish Pioneers and Patriots*, (Philadelphia: 1942), pp. 235ff. Rebecca and her husband, Henry Johnston, returned to England to live. In 1816, they were visited by General Winfield Scott, who noted that "she had become from bad health prematurely old . . . Taking a sudden turn, she exclaimed, with emphasis: 'I have gloried in my rebel countrymen!' Then pointing to Heaven, with both hands, she added, in a most affecting tone: 'Would to God I, too, had been a patriot.'" *Ibid*, p. 243.

2. Morris occasionally handled goods for the government. He sold tobacco captured at Yorktown for a net gain of $13,109. On commercial transactions valued at $99,027, he had profits of $21,881 and losses of $10,915, for a net gain to the United States of $10,966. *See* William Graham Sumner, *The Financier and the Finances of the American Revolution* (NY: 1891, 1970), vol. 2, p. 127.

3. Wolf and Whiteman, *History of the Jews of Philadelphia*, p. 120. Or the scroll might have been given later. Either speculation is based on future events: In 1825, there was an argument between Barrow E. Cohen and the officers of Shearith Israel. Salomon's son, Haym M., sided with Cohen. This led to the formation of another New York congregation, Bnai Jeshurun. At that point, Haym M., wrote to Zalegman Phillips, the parnas of Mickveh Israel. In the letter, dated June 23, 1825, Salomon mentioned that his father's scroll was "so dimned the Ink of its writing that in many places it has become quite obscure," and he insisted on its immediate return. Phillips replied that the scroll was in good condition and that he wouldn't return it. Salomon wrote back on November 30: "I need not remind you how indifferent after his Haym Salomon's death his survivors were in keeping up a regular attendance on the shull." *Ibid*, p. 257.

4. On October 22, 1782, Nones published a reply in the *Gazetteer*, saying he was shocked at Levy's accusations. He added that on October 9, he had been accosted by Abraham Levy on the street. Nones had been rude, for which he apologized; witnessed by Moses Cohen and Ephraim Clark. November 9, Ezekiel Levy replied to Nones. November 12, Nones replied, saying of the Levy's: "They hugged themselves, no doubt, in the satisfactory reflection of their own cunning by which they had bilked me of the commissions they promised."

5. Chaloner, worth £61,600 in 1780, had one horse and one slave listed in the tax records of 1783. June 14, 1783, he advertised merchandise for sale in the *Gazetteer*. His store was on Chestnut Street at the corner of Third. January 17, 1784, he was listed in the *Gazetteer* as being on the Committee of Vestry for Christ's Church and St. Peter's Church.

6. Bank dividends averaged 8 3/4 percent in 1782, 14½ percent in 1783, 13½ percent in 1784, and 6 percent in 1785. Dividends were announced in the papers, such as this ad in the *Gazetteer* of January 10, 1784:

Bank of North-America,
Philadelphia, January 5, 1784.
The Directors of the Bank having declared a dividend of eight per cent, upon the capital stock for the half year, ending the first instant, the same will be paid at the Bank to the stockholder . . .

The United States received $22,867 in dividends, paying back $29,719 in interest on loans.

7. Eleazer Levy had had the mortgage on the land the army took over for Westpoint fort. Levy was never repaid. Wolf and Whiteman, *History of the Jews of Philadelphia*, p. 419 n.

# Notes

8. Cited in Charles E. Russell, *Haym Salomon and the Revolution*, (NY: 1930), pp. 203, 204, 246. Russell was quoting figures from Salomon's estate inventory. Unfortunately, there are no exact dates given. Charles Armand Tufin, the Marquis de la Rouarie, had originally recruited his legion on a Congressional appropriation of $94,000 in 1779. A year later, he had the misfortune of serving with Gates at Camden. Morris doled out warrants totaling $6,445 22/90 to Armand on February 5, 10 and March 28, 29, 1783. Arthur St. Clair was not, personally, in need. In 1783, he had three horses and a cow and in 1784, he was licensed as an auctioneer. February 28, 1784, he advertised in the *Gazetteer* as Arthur St. Clair & Co. with John Patton and David Lenox. The office was on Front Street, above Walnut. It should be pointed out that Salomon was paying in Pennsylvania currency.

## VI. An Army of Creditors

1. In the *Packet* of February 7, 1784, Salomon was listed as not having paid his taxes:

| North Ward | State Money · | | | Specie | | |
|---|---|---|---|---|---|---|
| A vacant lot, said to belong to Haym Solomon's estate | £1 | 5 | 9 | £7 | 12 | 5 |

2. Asher Myers had been parnas of Shearith Israel in 1765 and 1771.

3. Given as Lieut. Col. John Shee and Capt. Joseph Greenway in *The Pennsylvania Archives*, Robert McAfee, ed. (Harrisburg: 1906), series 6, vol. 1, p. 101. Hyim Solomon, Solomon Lyons and Mosses Jacobs are listed as Greenway privates in *The Pennsylvania Archives*, vol. 3, part 2, p. 1287. Jonas Phillips had joined Capt. John Linton's Company in Col. William Bradford's Battalion (Oct. 31, 1778). Isaac Moses was a private along with Solomon Myers Cohen in Capt. Andrew Burkhard's Company in Col. William Will's Battalion (1780). Simon Nathan was in Capt. Andrew Geyer's 3rd Company in Col. Will's Battalion. Philip Moses Russel had served as a surgeon's mate under Gen. Lee in 1775, spent the winter of 1777–78 at Valley Forge as mate to Dr. Norman of the 2nd Virginia Regiment, and then resigned in 1780 due to ill health.

4. Morris repaid Salomon on September 23, 1783.

5. Nathans' first ad as a broker appeared in the *Gazetteer*, August 21, 1784. He had an office in Front Street, nine doors above Market, "where Mr. Rice's book-store was kept."

6. The parting of the soldiers ironically recalls the original proposals for

a seal of the United States. In July, 1776, Franklin, Adams and Jefferson had been appointed to assess designs. Franklin favored "Moses standing on the shore, and extending his Hand over the sea, thereby causing the same to overwhelm Pharoah who is sitting in an open Chariot ... Rays from a Pillar of Fire in the Clouds, reaching to Moses, to express that he acts by Command of the Deity. Motto, *Rebellion to Tyrants Is Obedience to God*." Jefferson preferred the Jews passing through the Red Sea. The recommendations were tabled only to be reenacted seven years later.

7. There were eight hundred signers, among them Moses Cohen, Isaac Franks, Seymour Hart, Isaac Levy, Moses Levy, Isaac Moses and Jonas Phillips.

8. Adams felt that he, and not Morris, Franklin, or the French, was responsible for the loans and credits which were received by government coffers during this period.

## VII. Jews, Politics and Business

1. Jews could not become citizens until 1740, when King George II, celebrating his thirteenth year as king, issued "An Act for naturalizing such foreign Protestants and others therein mentioned, as are settled or shall settle, in any of His Majesty's Colonies in America." Protestants, Quakers and Jews, but not Catholics, could become citizens after living in the colonies for at least seven years and pledging allegiance to the King. On the opposite side of the Channel, the Holy Roman Emperor, Joseph II, issued a *Toleranzpatent* in 1781, granting privileges to Protestants and Jews.

2. The New York constitution, which was typical of those in other states, established an assembly and senate (the legislature), and a governor and Supreme Court (the council). It retained the British Chancery Court. Voting was based on age and property. For the assembly, one had to have a freehold worth £20, or rent a tenement of 40 shillings per year value, and pay taxes. For the senate, minimum worth for the freehold was £100. The same values held for those running for elective office. The oath of allegiance did not have to be taken by Quakers, who needed only to give "affirmation."

3. *Gazetteer*, January 10, 1784.

4. *Gazetteer*, February 14, 1784:

### PROPOSALS

For establishing another Bank by subscription in the city of Philadelphia, by the name of

The BANK of Pennsylvania. The utility of the Bank of North-America, established in this city, has been so manifest,

as to induce the subscribers to offer to their fellow citizens the
following plan of raising another, as nearly similar to it as shall
be found proper, in order that the benefits arising therefrom
may be extended to a great length than one institution of that
kind can be expected to reach to . . .

January 19, 1784

Seven hundred shares of $400 Spanish milled each would be sold. A meeting
was called for selecting a president and directors, and for writing a constitution. Subscription papers were held by Samuel Howell, Archibald M'Call,
John Bayard, Edward Shippen, George Emlen, Jared Ingersol, Thomas
Fisher, John Steinmetz, Tench Coxe, David Rittenhouse, Samuel Pleasants,
Joseph Swift, Jeremiah Warder, Peter Knight, and Robert Knox. Salomon
had had recent dealings with Coxe concerning a number of bills Salomon was
selling for Morris.

5. A committee on the Bank of North America was appointed. Its
members were Thomas Willing, Thomas Fitzsimmons, James Wilson and
Gouvernor Morris. They explained through ads that the people who had
already bought stock at $500 a share could either apply the $100 difference to
new shares, or receive the $100, adjusted upwards at an annual interest rate
of 6 percent, back.

6. Wolf and Whiteman, *History of the Jews of Philadelphia*, pp. 110-13,
discuss this. They feel Salomon wrote the reply with the help of Eleazer
Oswald, printer of the *Gazetteer*, merchant and seller of stationery.

7. Livingston was born in New York City in 1746. He attended King's
College, now known as Columbia, and went on to become a lawyer and
delegate to the Continental Congress. He helped draft the New York state
constitution and was appointed the first chancellor of the state.

## VIII. Jews and Freemasonry

1. Like masons, some Sons of Liberty groups used a secret language and
wore medals, such as a medallion showing a liberty pole and liberty tree.

2. Lodge No. 2, F. & A.M. was formed around 1760. It was Ancient or
Atholl. The meeting place was Videll's Lodge Alley on Second Street, below
Chestnut, except for during the British occupation, when the lodge moved to
the City Tavern at Second Street and Gold. Meetings were held frequently,
but few members attended with regularity. The minutes were usually kept by
Annon Lucis (A.L.), and 4,000 years was added to the date. 4,000 B.C.
represented the Year of Light, when the world began. Anno Mundi (A.M.)
was used in the Scottish Rite and was the same as Anno Hebraico. This was

computed by adding 3760 to the date. Meetings were divided according to the event: an E.A. Lodge meant someone was going to become an Entered Apprentice; F.C. Lodge meant Fellow Craft; and so on. R.W.G.M. was always abbreviated, even in speech. There was another Solomon who was a mason; he visited the lodge May 12, 1767. As for secrecy, see *The New-York Journal or The General Advertiser*, September 1, 1768: "Just published ... HIRAM: OR THE GRAND MASTER — KEY TO THE DOOR OF BOTH ANCIENT AND MODERN FREE-MASONRY, Being an accurate Description of every Degree ... By a Member of Royal Arch."

3. As a Master-elect, Salomon was probably read the "Antient Charges and Regulations" which demanded he be a good man, obey the moral law, and avoid excess. After being raised, Salomon paid dues of between $50 and $60 for the year.

4. William Dinslow, *10,000 Famous Freemasons*; Ronald Heaton, *Masonic Membership of the Founding Fathers*, (Washington, D.C.: 1965); Norris Barrat and Julius Sachse, *Freemasonry in Pennsylvania 1727–1907*, (Philadelphia: 1908), vols. 1, 2.

5. If there was money left over, another balloon, 10 feet high and 20 feet in diameter, was planned. Other daring subscribers were Benjamin Nones, Miers Fisher, Jonas Phillips, Eleazer Oswald, John Chaloner and John Swanwick. See *The Packet*, June 29, 1784; *The Gazetteer*, July 31, 1784.

6. "A Haym Salomon Letter to Rabbi David Tevele Schiff, London, 1784," trans. Hyman B. Grinstein, *Publications of the American Jewish Historical Society*, no. 34, 1937. Grinstein mistakenly believed that both the rabbi and the heir lived in London, since the letter was addressed there.

7. *Minutes* of Shearith Israel. Gershom Seixas had returned to Shearith Israel in early February, 1784, writing Mickveh Israel from New York: "I have engaged to return to New York." His contract gave him £200 New York currency a year, six cords of hickory wood, matsoh, and "perquisites." His first sermon, delivered in English, spoke of the congregation's lack of decency and decorum.

8. The society did not formally start until after Salomon's death. Mordecai was gabay (treasurer). It lasted five years.

### Epilogue: An Intestate Fiasco

1. State Supreme Courts held jury trials. The Court for the Correction of Errors was composed of the president of the state senate, senators and the chancellor. The Court of Chancery was a holdover from the British, and was composed of chancellors and the governor.

2. According to Russell, *Haym Salomon*, p. 273, Salomon's Philadelphia

*Notes*

estate included $353,729.33 worth of loan office, treasury, commissioners' and Virginia State certifications, plus a substantial amount of Continental dollars. Translated into specie at market value, the estate was worth $40,945. The final inventory of 1789 showed assets of $44,732 and debts of $45,292.

3. Cited in Wolf and Whiteman, *History of the Jews of Philadelphia*, p. 137. Josephson was a broker. A similar matter arose at Shearith Israel. The "List of Debts Due to the Sedaka of K.K. Shearith Israel, Nisan 8th, 5547" shows Hyam Solomons owing 5.7.6. Jacob Mordecai owed 24.13.6. A year later, the "Account of Monies recd for Offerings to the Tsedeka" showed a contribution from Haim Solomons. Presumably, Levy or Rachel contributed that.

4. Haym M. had taken the stance that his father was a creditor of the government. When Secretary of the Treasury Alexander Hamilton had delivered the first report on the public credit to Congress, January 14, 1790, he had quoted Article VI, Section 1 of the Constitution, that "all debts contracted, and engagements entered into, before the adoption of that Constitution, shall be as valid against the United States under it as under the Confederation." Hamilton had insisted that the article applied to the Congressional circular of 1783, which listed a class of creditors who had either loaned some portion of their funds or property to the government, or accepted some portion of the government debt as their own. The national government, Hamilton had stated, must now fund the national debt. Congress had debated the report: Jefferson and Madison were against it, since it diluted state power; Benjamin Rush wrote Congressman Thomas Fitzsimmons that "the whole profits of the war will soon center in the hands of American Tories, Amsterdam Jews, and London brokers, while the brave men who deserved them will end their lives in jails and hospitals or beg the bread ..."

It was a strangely mixed prophecy. Part of the debate had centered on whether to cancel the foreign debt, which was approximately $11,710,378. That would have served to isolate American trade and would have exacerbated events at a time when relations to Britain and France were already becoming tense. The domestic debt was $40,414,086. Hamilton had emphasized the payment of treasury and state securities, putting aside Continental currency, most loan office certificates, and most notes.

5. Salomon, towards the end of his life, had tried to have Phillips excommunicated.

# Bibliography

## Archives and Collections

Historical Society of Pennsylvania. The T. Coxe–H. Salomon Papers.

New York Public Library, Rare Books Division. Books and Pamphlets:

*The Balloting Book, and other Documents Relating to Military Bounty Lands, in the State of New York.* New York: Printed by Packard & Van Benthuysen, 1825.

*A Committee of Twenty-five.* New York, 1774.

The Constitution of the State of New York. Printed by Samuel London. New York: 1777.

The Constitution of the State of New York. Reprinted by E. Holt. New York: 1785.

*A Copy of the Poll List of the Election for Representatives for the City and County of NEW-YORK.* 1769.

Deane, Silas. *An Address to the Free and Independent Citizens of the United States of North-America.* Hartford: Printed by Hudson & Goodwin, 1784.

Low, John. *An Alphabetical Table of the Situation and Extent of the Different Streets, Roads, Lanes, etc. of the City of New York.* New York: 1807.

Morris, Robert. *Account of Robert Morris' Property*. 1803.

Morris, Robert. *A Plan for Liquidating Certain Debts of the State of Pennsylvania*. December, 1785.

Morris, Robert. *A Statement of the Accounts of the United States of America During the Administration of the Superintendant of Finance*. Philadelphia: Printed by Robert Aitken, 1785.

*New York City Census*, 1806.

Slade, William. *Masonic Penalties*. Vermont: Printed by H.H. Houghton, 1830.

*State of the Four Regiments Raised in the Colony of New York* ... Jacob Blackwell, Chairman. August 4, 1775.

New York Public Library, Rare Books Division. Newspapers:
*The Daily Advertiser*
*The Independent Gazetteer or, The Chronicle of Freedom*
*The New-York Gazette*
*The New-York Gazette and the Weekly Mercury*
*The New-York Journal; or, The General Advertiser*
*The New-York Journal and State Gazette*
*The Pennsylvania Journal and Weekly Advertiser*
*The Pennsylvania Packet*
*The Pennsylvania Packet, and Daily Advertiser*
*The Royal Gazette*

New York Public Library. Manuscript Division.
Robert Morris Papers
Haym Salomon Papers

Pennsylvania Archives (Harrisburg Publishing Co.).
Series 3. William Henry Egle, ed. 1897.
Series 6. Robert McAfee, ed. 1906.

The Supreme Court Archives of New York State. Includes Chancery, Court for Correction of Errors, Mayor's Court Minutes.

Surrogate's Court, New York, New York.
Letter of Administration, July 20, 1785. Liber 2, 333
Conveyances: March 8, 1794. Liber 49, 424–427.
March 10, 1794. Liber 49, 427–429.
June 18, 1811. Liber 92, 406.
Letter of Administration, May 30, 1821. Liber 18, 92.

Yivo Institute, New York, New York. Minutes of Congregation Shearith Israel.

## Articles

Baer, Frank L. "The First Subscribers to the Bank of North America." *National Genealogical Society Quarterly* 57, no. 4 (Dec. 1969).

Barzilay, Isaac E. "The Jew in the Literature of the Enlightenment." *Jewish Social Studies* 18, no. 4 (Oct. 1956).

Blau, Joseph L. "Some Historical Facts of Jewish Affiliation." *Jewish Social Studies* 31, no. 3 (July 1969).

Duker, Abraham G. "Polish Frankism's Duration." *Jewish Social Studies* 25, no. 4 (Oct. 1963).

Grinstein, Hyman B. "A Haym Salomon Letter to Rabbi David Tevele Schiff, London, 1784." *Publications of the American Jewish Historical Society* no. 34 (1937).

Hühner, Leon. "Naturalization of Jews in New York Under the Act of 1740." *Publications of the American Jewish Historical Society* no. 13 (1905).

James, Cyril F. "The Bank of North America." *The Pennsylvania Magazine* 64, no. 1 (Jan. 1940).

Kohler, Max I. "Phases of Jewish Life in New York Before 1800." *Publications of the American Jewish Historical Society* no. 2 (1894).

"The Lyons Collection." *Publications of the American Jewish Historical Society* no. 27 (1920).

Morais, Rev. Sabato. "Mickve Israel Congregation of Philadelphia." *Publications of the American Jewish Historical Society* no. 1 (2d ed., 1905).

"Notes and Documents." *American Jewish Historical Quarterly* no. 40, parts 1–4 (Sept. 1950–June 1952).

"Pennsylvania Bank Subscribers." List appearing in *Daughters of the American Revolution Magazine* 103, no. 8 (Oct. 1969): 725.

Pool, David de Sola. "Reminiscences of Former Days." *American Jewish Historical Quarterly* 52, no. 1 (Sept. 1962).

Sparks, Jared. "A Sketch of Haym Salomon from an Unpublished Ms. in the Papers of Jared Sparks." *Publications of the American Jewish Historical Society* no. 2 (1894).

Stern, Malcolm H. "Jewish Marriage and Intermarriage in the Federal Period." *American Jewish Archives* 19, no. 2 (Nov. 1967).

Vaxer, Menasseh. "Naturalization Roll of Jews of New York (1740–1759)." *American Jewish Historical Quarterly* no. 40, parts 1–4 (Sept. 1950–June 1952).

Walsh, James J. "The Chevalier de La Luzerne." *Records of the American Catholic Historical Society of Philadelphia* 16 (1905).

# Books

Alberts, Robert C. *The Golden Voyage: The Life and Times of William Bingham (1752–1804)*. Boston: Houghton Mifflin, 1969.

*The Annals of America*. Vols. 1, 2, 3. Chicago: Encyclopaedia Britannica, Inc., 1968.

Baron, H.S. *Haym Salomon: Immigrant and Financier of the American Revolution*. New York: Bloch, 1929.

Barrat, Norris, and Sachse, Julius. *Freemasonry in Pennsylvania 1727–1907*. Vols. 1, 2. Philadelphia: New Era Printing, 1908.

Coil, Henry W. *A Comprehensive View of Freemasonry*. New York: MaCoy, 1954.

*The Confidential Correspondence of Robert Morris*. Philadelphia: Stan. V. Henkels, Auction Commission, 1917.

Conway, Moncure D. *Omitted Chapters of History Disclosed in the Life and Papers of Edmund Randolph*. New York: Da Capo Press, 1971.

Dawson, Henry B. *The Sons of Liberty in New York*. Reprint. New York: Arno Press and the New York Times, 1969.

Dimont, Max I. *Jews, God and History*. New York: New American Library, 1962.

Dinslow, William R. *10,000 Famous Freemasons*.

Dubnow, S.M. *History of the Jews in Russia and Poland*. Trans. J. Friedlander. Philadelphia: Jewish Publication Society of America, 1916.

Elmaleh, Rev. L.H., and Samuel, J. Bunford. *The Jewish Cemetery Ninth and Spruce Streets, Philadelphia*. May, 1906.

*Encyclopaedia Judaica*. Vol. 11. Jerusalem: MacMillin, 1971.

Fast, Howard. *Haym Salomon: Son of Liberty*. New York: Julian Messner, 1941.

Ferguson, E. James. *The Power of the Purse*. Chapel Hill: The University of North Carolina Press, 1961.

Friedman, Lee M. *Jewish Pioneers and Patriots*. Philadelphia: The Jewish Publication Society of America, 1942.

Heaton, Bro. Ronald E. *Masonic Membership of the Founding Fathers*. Washington, D.C.: The Masonic Service Association, 1965.

Hertzberg, Arthur, ed. *Judaism*. New York: George Braziller, 1962.

Homes, Henry A., ed. *Description and Analysis of the Remarkable Collection of Unpublished Manuscripts of Robert Morris*. Albany, N.Y.: Joel Munsell, 1876.

# Bibliography

Horsmanden, Daniel. *The New York Conspiracy*. Ed. Thomas J. Davis. Boston: Beacon, 1971.

Hutchinson, W.T., and Rachal, W.M., eds. *The Papers of James Madison*. Vols. 4, 5. Chicago: The University of Chicago Press, 1967.

*The Jewish Encyclopedia*. Ed. Isidore Singer. Vol. 8. New York: Funk and Wagnalls, 1904, 1925.

Kohler, Max. *Haym Salomon, The Patriot Broker of the Revolution: His Real Achievements and their Exaggeration. An Open Letter to Congressman Celler*. 1931.

Lewin, Louis. *Geschichte der Juden in Lissa*. Pinne: N. Gundermann, 1904.

Lewis, Lawrence. *A History of the Bank of North America*. Philadelphia: D.B. Lippincott, 1882.

McAdam, D., et al., eds. *History of the Bench and Bar of New York:* New York History Co., 1897.

Madison, Charles A. *Eminent American Jews 1776 to the Present*. New York: Frederick Ungar, 1970.

*Memoirs of the Marshall Count de Rochambeau*. Originally trans. M.W.S. Wright, printed 1838. Reprint. New York: The New York Times and Arno Press, 1971.

Morais, Henry S. *The Jews of Philadelphia*. Philadelphia: The Levytype Co., 1894.

Morse, Sidney. *Freemasonry in the American Revolution*. Washington, D.C.: The Masonic Service Ass'n of the United States, 1924.

New York Comptroller's Office. *New York in the Revolution*. Vols. 1, 2. New York: J.B. Lyon, 1904.

Peters, Madison C. *The Jews in America*. New York: John C. Winston, 1905.

Pool, Rev. D. De Sola. *The Mill Street Synagogue 1730–1817 of the Congregation Shearith Israel*. New York: 1930.

_____. *Portraits Etched in Stone*. New York: Columbia University Press, 1952.

_____, and Pool, Tamar de Sola. *An Old Faith in the New World*. New York: Columbia University Press, 1955.

Ramsey, L.G.G., ed. *The Complete Encyclopedia of Antiques*. New York: Hawthorn, 1962.

Robinson, Henry James. *The Power of the Purse*. London: John Murray, 1928.

163

Rupp, I. Daniel. *A Collection of Upwards of Thirty Thousand Names of . . . Immigrants in Pennsylvania 1727–1776.* Baltimore: Genealogical Publishing Co., 1965.

Russell, Charles Edward. *Haym Salomon and the Revolution.* New York: Cosmopolitan, 1930.

Schappes, Morris U., ed. *A Documentary History of the Jews in the United States 1654–1875.* New York: Citadel, 1950, 1952.

Shadwell, Col., and Clerke, H., eds. *Constitutions of the Antient Fraternity of Free and Accepted Masons Under the United Grand Lodge of England.* London: Harrison and Sons, 1884.

Sharp, Samuel L. *Poland: White Eagle on a Red Field.* Cambridge: Harvard University Press, 1953.

Sparks, Jared, ed. *Diplomatic Correspondence.* Vols. 1, 2. Washington, D.C.: United States Department of State.

Steeg, Clarence L. Ver. *Robert Morris: Revolutionary Financier.* Philadelphia: University of Pennsylvania Press, 1954.

Sumner, William Graham. *The Financier and the Finances of the American Revolution.* Vol. 2. New York: Burt Franklin, 1891, 1970.

Swiggett, Howard. *The Extraordinary Mr. Morris.* New York: Doubleday, 1952.

Vaughan, Alden T., ed. *Chronicles of the American Revolution.* Originally compiled by Hezekia Niles. New York: Grosset & Dunlap, 1965.

Wharton, Francis, ed. *The Revolutionary Correspondence of the United States.* Washington, D.C.: Government Printing Office, 1889.

Wolf, Edwin, and Whiteman, Maxwell. *The History of the Jews of Philadelphia from Colonial Times to the Age of Jackson.* Philadelphia: The Jewish Publication Society of America, 1957.

# Index

165

# Index

New York Assembly 22
New York City 9, 14, 15, 27; British occupation 12, 25, 27, 92, 94; Dutch settlement 8, 14, 15; and Jewish population 14, 15; Jews' alley 15, 16 *see also* Shearith Israel
Newport 16, 26; Jewish community 16; synagogue (Jeshuat Israel) 16
Newton, Sir Isaac 20 *see also* finances
Nixon, John 37, 42, 45
Nones, Benjamin 69, 70, 74, 93, 106, 118
nonimportation resolution 11, 57
Norris, Isaac 17, 56
Nourse, Joseph 61, 121, 122

Ord (Captain) 41
Osgood, Samuel 44
Oswald, Eleazer 111, 112

Paine, Thomas 88
Parker, Daniel, & Co. 97
partition 7, 53 *see also* Poland
Paterson, John 123
paymaster general notes *see* finances
*Pear Tree (de Pereboom)* 14
Penn, William 92
Pennsylvania Bank 39, 42 *see also* banking, finances, Robert Morris
Pennsylvania Committee of Safety 40
Pennsylvania General Assembly: oath 94; 1764 election 8
Pentateuch 9
Percy 11
Peter Whitesides & Co. 41
Peters, Richard 42
*Phila* 17

Philadelphia: Jewish cemetery 17, 113–114; and Jews 56, 57, 59; occupation 26, 27, 57; 1780 tax list 34–35
Phillips, Jonas 11, 31, 36–37, 53, 58, 59, 93–94, 95, 106, 123
Pinto, Isaac 16
Pinto, Joseph Jessurum 16
Poland: Alexander Josef v. Sulkowski 7; Council of Four Lands 6; General Confederacy 7; messianic movements 7; partition 7, 53; relation to Jews 6, 53, 73; taxation 6, 7
Polheymus, Dominie Johannes Theodorus 14
Pope Clement XII 103
Pope Innocent III 26
Popham, William 50
privateer, privateering 33, 41, 42, 69; defined 33; letters of Marque and Reprisal 33; participants 33, 41, 42, 69
profiteer, profiteering 33, 59, 66; defined 33; participants 59
Provost, David 15
Provost 12 *see also* William Cunningham
Putnam, Israel 9

Randolph, Edmund 65, 75
Rendon, Don Francisco 56
Reuveni 7 *see also* Poland
Revere, Paul 105
Revolution: army 24, 43, 76, 84–86, 87; blockade 53, 59, 64; Brooklyn Heights 9, 11; Fort Ticonderoga 26; Harlem Heights 11; Kipp's Bay 11, 12; Long Island 9, 11; nonimportation resolution 11; peace 77, 92; reasons for 9; relationship with France 22, 43, 60, 74, 75; St. John's Fort 18; Saratoga 26;

Ticonderoga *see* Fort Ticonderoga
Tilton, James 24
Tongue, William 12, 13
Touro, Rabbi Isaac de Abraham
16, 106
Townshend Acts 11
Treville 19
Turnball, William, & Co. 41

Vanderkele 90
Vanderlockt, William 77, 84
van Swellem, Asser Levy 15
Verdier (Captain) 69
Ver Planck, Guilian 121
Vergennes, Charles Gravier
(Comte de) 22, 75
von Heister 11, 12
von Sulkowski, Alexander Josef 7

Walker, Joseph 108
Wallace, John 123
Wallace, Joshua Maddax 97
Walsh (General) 71
Washington, George 9, 11, 17, 45,
46, 54, 60, 69, 70, 122, 123; and

the army 43, 46, 50; and
masonry 105; and Robert Mor-
ris 41, 46, 48, 50, 54 *see also*
masonry, masons, Robert Mor-
ris, finances, Revolution
Watson & Cossoul 73, 76
Watts, John 121
Webb 104
Westpoint Fort 70
White (Bishop) 123
White, Mary 39
Wilcox, John 95
Willet, Marinus 120, 121
Willing, Charles 37
Willing, Thomas 37, 39, 42, 54,
123
Willing & Morris 36, 37, 39–40,
41, 123
Wilson, James 37, 39, 42, 81, 82,
84, 123
Wragg, Elizabeth 19

Yorktown *see* Revolution

Zuntz, Alexander 83, 123